SOLVING QUALITY AND PRODUCTIVITY PROBLEMS: GOODMEASURE'S GUIDE TO CORRECTIVE ACTION

SOLVING QUALITY AND PRODUCTIVITY PROBLEMS: GOODMEASURE'S GUIDE TO CORRECTIVE ACTION

**by the Staff of Goodmeasure, Inc.
with an Introduction by Rosabeth Moss Kanter**

Contributors
Tana Pesso
David Summers
Rosabeth Moss Kanter
Barry Stein
Allan Cohen
Wendy D'Ambrose

ASQC Quality Press
American Society for Quality Control
310 West Wisconsin Avenue
Milwaukee, Wisconsin 53203

Published by ASQC Quality Press
Milwaukee

SOLVING QUALITY AND
PRODUCTIVITY PROBLEMS:
GOODMEASURE'S GUIDE TO
CORRECTIVE ACTION
by the Staff of Goodmeasure, Inc.

Acquisitions Editor: Jeanine L. Lau
Production Editor: Tammy Griffin
Cover Design: Artistic License
Set in Times by Artisan Graphics, Inc. Printed and bound by Edwards Brothers.

1098765432

ISBN 0-87389-043-4

Printed in the United States of America

Contributors

Tana Pesso was co-leader of the project team that developed Goodmeasure's approach to quality problem solving for a major multinational corporation. A specialist in enhancing the personal effectiveness of executives, she is a graduate of the Kennedy School of Government at Harvard.

David Summers, whose PhD is from Yale, served as a Goodmeasure director of research, writing about work alternatives and the practices of progressive companies.

Rosabeth Moss Kanter is the Class of 1960 Professor of Business Administration at the Harvard Business School. Among her nine books are *The Change Masters: Innovation and Entrepreneurship in the American Corporation, Men and Women of the Corporation*, and the just-published *Creating the Future* with Governor Michael Dukakis. She has been Chairman of the Board at Goodmeasure, Inc., and a consultant to leading companies around the world.

Barry Stein, President of Goodmeasure, Inc., specializes in the management of strategic change. He joined the consulting staff of Arthur D. Little after receiving engineering degrees from the Massachusetts Institute of Technology and has been advising major corporations ever since. He collaborated with Rosabeth Moss Kanter on *Life in Organizations*.

Allan Cohen, a Senior Vice President of Goodmeasure, is Professor and Chairman of the Management Department at Babson College. He wrote *Managing for Excellence* with David Bradford.

Wendy D'Ambrose is Vice President, Goodmeasure Enterprises, responsible for managing speakers and seminars.

Goodmeasure, Inc., is a management consulting firm headquartered in Cambridge, Mass., with an international clientele. Founded in 1977, its family of companies has grown to include a speakers service, a software firm, an audiovisual division, and affiliated consulting groups working to improve quality, leadership, innovation, and the management of change.

Contents

PART ONE
DEFINITIONS AND OVERVIEW

PART TWO
THE FIVE-STEP PROCESS

PART THREE
GETTING ORGANIZED FOR ACTION

PART FOUR
MANAGING TEAMS

PART ONE
DEFINITIONS AND OVERVIEW

Introduction

Quality Leadership and Change[*]
(*Rosabeth Moss Kanter*)

We are under siege as a nation, and many of our companies are under siege, because we're playing a very new game today. One thing I enjoy as I travel around the country, reminding people that the future is unfolding very differently from how we had imagined, is asking executives what game they think best describes their business today. We use many sports metaphors in business, so I've asked people to think about the right metaphor. The answers have been very interesting and very revealing.

At Apple Computer last summer, somebody said roller derby. At Bell South Corporation, an executive said he thought they were playing badminton in a hurricane. It's delicate, and they thought they had the skills, but storms were brewing all around them. In fact, another executive in the same company said he feared that he didn't even know what game they were playing. He was afraid his team would show up with five players and a big ball and the other team would show up fielding nine players and a little ball, and they wouldn't be able to win because they were playing the wrong game.

In considering the relationship of the environment to the dramatic need for quality, innovation, and better management in American corporations, I think the game that best describes most businesses today is the croquet game in *Alice in Wonderland*. In that game nothing remains stable for very long. Everything is changing around the players. Alice goes to hit the ball, but her mallet is a flamingo. Just as she's about to hit the ball, the flamingo lifts its head and looks in another direction. That's just like technology and the tools we use. Just when employees have mastered them, they seem to change, requiring different learning and competence.

When Alice finally thinks she's mastered the flamingo and goes to hit the ball, the ball becomes a hedgehog. It walks to another part of the court. That's just like our employees and customers, who are no longer waiting for us to whack them. Instead, they have minds of their own and will in fact walk off to another part of the court to choose another option in a heightened competitive environment.

And finally in that croquet game, the wickets are the card soldiers being ordered around by the Red Queen. This is perhaps a great metaphor for government.

---

*This article originally appeared in *Quality Progress* magazine in February 1987.

1

Just as Alice thinks she understands the tools, her employees, and her customers, the Red Queen barks out another order and the wickets reposition themselves. The very structure of industry, the structure of regulation, the structure of international competition, are changing at the same time that we're trying to get people to do a better job. That, to me, is the ultimate quality challenge. It's not only to improve what we're already doing, but it's to build into our organizations the capacity to improve and change direction as conditions change all around us.

That means paying attention not only to the visible mistakes, but also to the invisible mistakes. Randall Meyer, president of Exxon U.S.A., pointed this out to his people as an important distinction. He said most of what American industry pays attention to are the visible mistakes — solving problems and taking care of the processes that are under our control. What worries him for the future of industry and competitiveness are the invisible mistakes — missed opportunities. I was delighted to see in Westinghouse's statement of quality principles the statement that an important source of waste is the failure to exploit a technological opportunity or use a new tool or technique. I'm concerned with teaching organizations not only to avoid visible mistakes, waste, and failures, but also to avoid invisible mistakes. There are times when people have an idea about how to do something differently or better, to respond to a rapidly changing competitive environment, but they don't act on it.

I'd like to talk about the kind of people who do act on opportunities for change; in fact, have confidence in change. I call them *change masters*. These are the people who can see the need for, and lead, productive change. It could be the employees in a quality circle, it could be a hidden entrepreneur in middle management, it could be the chief executive or a staff department, or a customer-company coalition. There are certain aspects of culture, structure, and organization that allow people to lead productive change — to make the improvements needed to win at the game of *Alice in Wonderland* croquet.

First, the organization must put in place the systems, practices, culture, and rewards that will encourage people to be enterprising — to solve problems and to see and take advantage of opportunities. The first key is in how we define and organize around jobs. There's more initiative and enterprise in organizations that define jobs in broad, rather than narrow, terms. This idea is almost a cliche of modern management theory, yet it's a relatively newer idea for most organizations. The old wisdom about the best way to design jobs was that they should be as narrow and as specialized as possible, to avoid human error. People could do the same thing over and over again, getting better and better, and avoiding mistakes. Exceptions or problems were sent upward for management to take care of, or to another department.

The new wisdom says that people work better when they get bigger pieces to do or are connected more broadly to goals. The new wisdom about defining jobs says that there should be bigger pieces, clearer knowledge of goals, and measurement on results, not on rules. That's hard for very old organizations to do. In fact, it's much easier to put in a quality circle that takes people off the job than it is to change the definition of the job. Sometimes that's because of constraints built into the system. One concession that GM had to get from the UAW when it started New United Motors Manufacturing Inc., a joint venture with Toyota, concerned job classifications. In one major area, when GM ran that plant, they had over 35 job classifications. The Japanese had only three — all bigger, all broader, all tappng people's enterprise, by giving them a bigger piece of the picture to pay attention to.

One of our leading consumer goods manufacturers, one that gets high marks on quality from consumers, has been very successful with a new work design system that involves one job classification. Now, almost 50 percent of their plants have systems in which jobs and responsibilities are enlarged and broadened. Employee teams manage their piece of the business as if they owned it. In the most advanced example of that system, costs are about 50 percent of what they are in a conventional plant, quality is much higher, and they have reduced the need for supervision down to 17 managers for about 350 people. They really need only four managers — one plant manager and one product manager for each of the three product lines. They still have 17 because the employees don't want to see the middle managers done out of a job. But in fact, the plant could run effectively with just employees in teams who have mastered all of the jobs. They're on a pay-for-knowledge system; as people master each job, their pay goes up. Seventy-five percent of the people are at the highest pay rate already because they've learned it all.

Some high-tech companies take this notion of broad job definition to an extreme. In some computer companies the typical job definition is, "Do the right thing." People are given no more guidelines than that. "We'll aim you in the right direction, but it's up to you to figure out how to get results." That's extreme — but the worst thing you could hear any employee say in any company is, "That's not my job." Many companies suffer because jobs are defined too narrowly, and people don't have any sense of the reasons for what they're doing.

The second characteristic of change master companies is that they have a structure that's built around small working teams. The teams have autonomy to act in local areas and are functionally complete. That is, they have representatives from every function, every discipline, that's required to get the end job done. It's the opposite of dividing the process into infinite numbers of departments and specialists, each with a territory to manage.

This is why, for a long time, Hewlett-Packard's classic growth strategy was "small is beautiful." As soon as a division grew to more than 2,000 people or reached $100 million in sales, they would break it into two divisions. That would produce a smaller business unit where integration across specialties and the ability to act locally were fostered. In that kind of structure, people take ownership for results. They can see the customer firsthand. In fact, there's a famous example

3

of an engine plant that makes truck engines, built around cross-functional teams. Whenever there's an accident involving a truck that uses its engines, representatives of the team responsible for that product visit the truck driver and his or her family. They take personal responsibility for the failures, as well as personal responsibility for the end product, because they're part of an integrated team.

The third noteworthy aspect of change master companies is in their culture. Those organizations that tap people's problem-solving abilities and enterprising skills have what I call a culture of pride, rather than a culture of mediocrity or inferiority. A culture of pride has several aspects. First is a myth that says, "Our people are the best people and they're always getting better." I say it's a myth because the number of high-tech companies, all in the same industry, each of which swears that it hires only from the top 5 percent of the class, tells me that it must be a statistical impossibility. But they all believe that they have only the best.

I contrast that with the attitude I see in companies that are not as good at innovation and are scrambling to keep up. In the results from employee opinion surveys, in response to the statement, "We hire only the best people," fewer than 20 percent of the employees show even weak agreement with that statement. That's a culture of inferiority or mediocrity. The belief is that if you've worked there for more than two years, you must be a real turkey.

In such companies, the attitude is that all wisdom comes from the outside, not from the inside. If you want to make a change, hire an outsider. In one insurance company, for example, the whole top management team had turned over within three years, and six out of the nine players were new to the company within two years. Every time they wanted a new function or a new department, they'd bring in somebody from Citicorp or IBM or GE, rather than look for people from the inside. They didn't believe they had the best people. They used consultants freely, and for trivia. I am not against using consultants — I should make that clear. But they should not substitute for things that people inside could do perfectly well. That insurance company actually hired consultants to figure out how to speed up the photocopying of procedures manuals. Wouldn't that have been a wonderful opportunity for a team of their own employees to become heroes by solving a problem?

We also recognize cultures of pride by their expenditures. High-innovation, flexible companies that are better at adapting to change spend more on human resource programs, on career development, and education in particular. Low-innovation companies — and by the way, this is based on statistical comparisons that were part of my research — do not necessarily avoid spending. Instead, they tend to spend on recruitment and replacement costs because of high turnover. On the other hand, high-innovation companies invest in things that will make their employees better over time. Increasingly, those investments, which tell people that they're valued and are getting better, are not done just at the point of promotion, which is the classical system. It's done simply to improve people's ability to take action in their current position, whether or not they were groomed for anything more. It assumes that people can always do more, regardless of whether they're moving up in the official hierarchy.

Another aspect of the culture of pride is in the abundant praise, recognition, awards, trophies, and wall plaques — all of which populates high-innovation companies. Like many of you, I greeted these at first with skepticism. I said, "What does this rah-rah culture really do for motivation? How many of us really work for a trophy or a plaque or a pat on the back?" I realized that the impact is not on the people who actually get the award, but on the others who view it. It's the publicity value from which the high-innovation companies benefit — the fact that everybody sees what our people are capable of. That raises the esteem of the whole organization.

My firm did an innovation audit on a company that wanted to know whether it had the systems and practices that would allow it to compete in the new game. We told them that among all the reasons why their product development was slow and not particularly exciting, was the fact that they didn't have much in the way of recognition systems. And they said, "But wait a minute, didn't we show you? Sure we do." It turned out that they did have a lot of awards, but they were all secret. People would get a little cash stuffed in the paycheck or the boss would do something in private. It defeated the whole purpose. It's the publicity value that creates a culture of pride in which everybody feels they must live up to the level of achievement set by the people who were singled out as role models.

And finally, we found that high-innovation companies have a different attitude toward reward. They not only have rewards that pay people after they do a good job, but they also have what I call investment-oriented rewards. These are rewards before the fact — investments in the fact that somebody will perform later. It might take the form of a budget for a special project, or a pool of cash that employees can tap if they write proposals and show that they had something good to do with it. Data General Corporation became famous through the bestseller, *Soul of a New Machine*. It described how a manager, Tom West, got teams of young engineers to perform miracles. They did in one year what the experts said would take five years or could never be done at all. They built a totally new computer from scratch — a computer, by the way, that along with its following generations is responsible for more than half of the company's total revenues. He did it by extraordinary teamwork in an atmosphere where rewards seemed to be investment-oriented.

When the young engineers were asked, "What was in it for you? Why did you kill yourself for this product when you didn't even get stock options at the end?"

The answer was "Pinball."

Pinball? "Yes," they said, "it's like playing pinball. If you win, you get a free game. You get a chance to do it again on your own terms. The reward comes from being singled out and invested in." That's a very different attitude toward rewards. Challenge — opportunity — is one of the greatest untapped potential rewards that most organizations have. It doesn't cost anything to give people opportunities, and yet it often pays off in problems solved and innovations developed.

While the first feature of change master companies is encouraging people to be enterprising in the first place, the second is making sure they have the tools to act on their ideas. That's a matter of empowerment — making sure that people have access to what I consider the three key power tools in any organization: information, support, and resources.

Change master companies tend to make more information more available to more people at more levels through more devices. These devices include oral and written communication. I'm amused by some of the examples in *In Search of Excellence,* which talks about the famous one-page memo that one company developed to reduce paperwork. Behind the scenes, managers spend weeks and weeks perfecting the one-page memo. One senior executive sent back a memo 17 times to be rewritten so that it would be in perfect one-page form. Why didn't he just go and talk to the person to whom the memo was being sent?

High-innovation companies emphasize immediate, direct communication in real time, to give people the information they need to act. This is why many leading manufacturing companies, like the consumer products company I mentioned earlier, invest heavily in microcomputers to make sure that people on the shop floor can get immediate product data. In fact, in one division of that company, the workers on the shop floor have product data that the brand managers themselves don't have. By the way, that is a flaw in their system — the brand managers should probably have it too. But they emphasize people getting timely information about what they're doing. For this reason, there will likely be more meetings in high-innovation, high-quality, change master companies — more groups convening to share information and compare notes.

I happen to be a fan of *USA Today.* I particularly like their color-coded weather map, on which you can see instantly what the weather is like in any part of the country. I was going to propose that they do a similar map of meeting density, so that on any day you could see where meetings are taking place around the country. My guess would be that you'd find most on Route 128 in Boston, Silicon Valley, Austin, and maybe Pittsburgh, now that I know so much about what Westinghouse is doing. The map would be densest in places where there is an emphasis on adjustment, improvement, and change — because wherever there's change, there's a need to share information.

The attitude toward open information that exists in high-innovation companies sometimes astonishes even me. For example, some organizations have open meeting policies, which say that anybody can attend any meeting, unless particular individuals are being discussed. Now, most people hate meetings and would be unlikely to take advantage of that policy. But the point is they don't want to limit access. A "need-to-know" policy is counterproductive during change. Instead, those organizations emphasize access — not forcing information on people, but access.

There was a classic story at Wang Laboratories of a new executive who had an office on the executive floor. All of the offices had glass walls, although they also had doors. The new executive was sitting in his office one day, trying to interview somebody that he wanted to hire. It was a little noisy out in the hall, so he closed his door. Dr. Wang himself came by and started walking back and forth, peering through the glass wall. After that happened six or seven times, the fellow finally got the idea. He got up and opened his door, and Dr. Wang stopped walking by. It was important there that everybody be able to hear everything. In fact, at one HP division that we studied, people who were working on budgets found that the library was the only place where there wouldn't be people peering over the shoulder-height partitions at what was on their desks.

This attitude is very different from those in low-innovation companies that are not adapting to change and are having problems competing on quality and productivity. In those companies, the attitude was that information was a weapon to be hoarded by departments that felt that they were excluded from information about what was happening in the organization. At one telephone company, for example — predivestiture — the field people complained that they couldn't get certain data from headquarters that they needed to run their operation. So they paid somebody to go out and get that data for them. And they made sure that headquarters could never see their data thereby diminishing the total value of that information to the system.

Another aspect of empowering people to act on their ideas is to make sure the organization permits collaboration so that people can build problem-solving coalitions. One aspect of building such an environment is sheer mobility. People must be able to move freely across areas and functions. What used to be called "unusual career moves" are common in high-innovation companies. That is, people's careers often take them across many different functions rather than up in one direction. They acquire more knowledge and contact with people all over the organization.

The mobility doesn't have to be career or job mobility. It also involves the movement of people to gather and solve problems together. High innovation companies also seem to have more conferences, more councils, more reasons to be gathering people together. In fact, those of you who fly through Boston's Logan airport, the next time you do, look at the board that lists commuter airlines as you enter the airport. There's a very interesting anomaly on the list. It's called Digital Helicopters, and that's not a new commuter airline. It's DEC's own in-house helicopter service that flies between 17 New England facilities on a regular basis. DEC people can get out and collaborate on solving problems that may go beyond the local area. Contrast that with the usual corporate jet that costs $2,000 an hour and is available only to the top 20 people. It's a very different attitude toward who needs to move easily to collaborate.

In fact, at one point DEC was worried about its travel costs, naturally, so it installed an elaborate teleconferencing facility to reduce the need to travel. What do you think happened to travel costs? They went up, because as more people could communicate, they found even more reasons why they should be getting together.

It's also true that there's more total collaboration where there's more employment security. It's hard for people to be enterprising or to support each other in changes when they're not sure who's going to last. Having a sense that there's a future makes it easier for people to invest in and plan for that future. People must feel they have a future if you want them to take responsibility for creating it.

In addition, an organization has more innovation and support when its people work well together and where there's more access up, down, and around the hierarchy. Several companies in Silicon Valley have Friday afternoon beer parties around the company swimming pool. That's the kind of thing they do out there. It serves an important function for companies that must be innovative and have everyone constantly collaborating on problem solving. When everyone's around the swimming pool in bathing suits, it's hard to stand on rank. Paunch is a great leveler! People at all levels are mixing. That's the issue — that people have access to each other, regardless of rank or status.

This is why one major bank was seriously considering eliminating titles. Eliminate titles in a bank — 35 levels of vice presidents? They felt that those status distinctions interfere with mobilizing groups to solve problems, and with someone who has an idea to get support for it. The whole bank hasn't eliminated officer titles yet, but its credit card division has, in favor of very broad functional titles. The titles describe the person's "home," but don't make rank or status such a barrier to access.

Contrast that again to a company that's struggling to change its culture. Every time a task force is formed, each department makes sure that the team has a representative of equal rank from each department, or they won't play. That game inhibits the people who want to recruit talent, because instead they have to recruit status. It used to be impossible in some companies to get more than two levels of the hierarchy together in the same room at the same time. I've been in meetings where we'd start talking about what was going on at another level, and I'd say something innocent like, "Why don't we invite them in?" And people would say, "No, no, we can't do that."

This still happens in the best companies. When we plan conferences for the top 50 or 100 people to go play golf in Florida and talk about new goals and culture changes, we often recommend the presence of people from many levels below. That would provide first-hand contact with key issues. But people would say, "No, that violates protocol," or "We're nervous about it." Several years ago, one of these companies innovated skip-level meetings. Level A could skip Level B and meet directly with Level C to find out what was going on. But since Level B wasn't present, it all ended up being Level B's fault, which was the squeezed middle manager again. And that still got only two levels of the organization in the same room at the same time.

Clearly, flattening hierarchies and removing barriers to access are important to improving people's problem-solving capacities.

Finally, high-innovation companies also tend to decentralize resources to make them more available for local problem solving. This means more general managers through smaller business units; more project teams that have budgets; special resource pools at lower levels, like internal venture capital banks; and internal pools of unallocated funds that people can tap to solve problems. In short, they make it easier for people to tap locally what they need to get things done.

Again, a division of one leading bank began experimenting to make resources available locally, and also to give people incentives to solve problems. Their smart idea was to let employees keep a portion of the cost savings, to invest in their department's activities. This was not gainsharing, so they could not take it home and buy VCRs. It was not money to take out of the company — it was invested in the company. Any department that saved money for the company got to keep a portion of it in its budget, as long as it was invested in a productive new activity. That was another way to make resources more available locally.

To do these things in many companies, the culture must be changed. The first requirement is a shared vision. Before improving quality or changing the culture or business direction, people at every level must understand and buy into the vision. Consider, for example, the Stanley Works, a 150-year-old tool manufacturer. It's always been known for high quality and high profitability. Now it's meeting the Pacific Rim challenge in many basic product lines. At Stanley Tools, every worker on the shop floor can tell you why they're moving in the direction in which they're moving. They understand the rationale and what it means to them. The vision is real for them and they buy into it. It's not just another set of marching orders from the top.

Second, there must be a management structure in place. One doesn't simply announce, "We want to change." Rather, you manage changes, and make a clearly identifiable set of people responsible for them.

A third factor is education and action tools. Having a management structure and the education are the two easiest things for companies to do, and they're very important.

Fourth is the need to encourage local innovations and experiments, rather than imposing a discipline on everyone. Let local units decide for themselves what it means to operate with high quality and high performance, and to innovate in ways that might serve as models for the rest of the organization. At the same time, the people at the top must be continually reviewing other policies, strategies, structures, and systems in the organization to make sure they're all compatible with the direction.

There must be good communication in all directions to assure that people learn from what's happening locally and that the policy decisions made at the top quickly reach the people who are taking action locally. And there must be new signals, symbols, and rewards that tell people, "We're serious and we're going to prove it by signalling it in a different way, such as who gets promoted or which new plant gets the business."

This kind of management of a total change effort takes leadership. There are at least four important leadership competencies that we must encourage in the people who run our enterprises, to make sure they're doing these things.

First, like all change masters, they must be tuned into the environment and connected with sources of data and problems, so that they know what and when to change.

Second, they must be able to use a style of thinking that I call kaleidoscopic thinking. This is the ability to challenge traditional beliefs, assumptions, and practices, to see whether things should be done differently today. Change masters think the way a kaleidoscope works. A kaleidoscope is just a device for seeing patterns. When you look through it, a set of fragments forms a pattern. But if you twist it, shake it, or change direction, the same fragments form an entirely different pattern. It's not reality that's fixed, but often our views of reality. Change masters can shake up and shuffle the pieces of the business, the array of departments, the systems we use, in many different ways. They can challenge their own beliefs and assumptions to move toward something new.

Third, change masters have a clear vision and communicate it. They actively believe in it and are committed to it.

Fourth, change master leaders build coalitions. They know how to create partnerships across areas, between suppliers and the company, with customers as joint ventures, and with the union. They reach out to embrace many parties because they realize that every change must be sold — because people can say no to it.

Overall, the kind of environment that drives change master companies can be called integrated. The culture and structure are integrative. Jobs are broad so territories overlap. People tend to be linked together in cross-functional teams, oriented toward the same end product. Communication flows freely and knits people together. Groups can form and reform with access to any part of the organization if that's what's needed to solve a problem. These organizations are flexible, but they're also connected by a shared vision that's set at the top.

The opposite environment, which destroys the ability to be competitive, is what I call segmentalism. Such systems chop the world into tiny pieces. The philosophy is, "Stay on your piece, learn that job and nothing else, take no responsibility for anything else." Department doesn't talk to department, level doesn't talk to level. There are systemic roadblocks to innovation, change, and problem solving. This could be called the elevator mentality. Elevators go up and down in narrow vertical channels. That's the mentality, instead of just saying to the guy in the next office, "Can we get together to form a team or solve this problem?" Departments act as fortresses rather than collaborators. Internal competition nearly killed our auto industry. Buick thought Cadillac was the enemy, not that they were knit together by common purpose and need to collaborate. GM's new structure says they're no longer divided by product.

Unfortunately, even in this day of searching for excellence and questing for quality, too many companies still operate the old way. I predict that the biggest limitation many of you will have in implementing your quality goals will come from organizational structures and practices that segment people. It will come from the interdepartmental issues that can't be solved through quality circles at one level. It will come from the barriers that exist between areas — not from a lack of teamwork or a failure of the processes. You can establish excellent participative processes and statistical process controls and then fail because the weight of the whole organization is still too divisive.

In the interest of equal time, I wrote a corporate philosophy for the company that prefers mediocrity and stagnation. This is my guide to *stifling innovation* for those who *do not* want to be change masters:

- Be suspicious of any new idea from below — because it's new and because it's from below. If the idea were any good, the people at the top would have thought of it already.
- Insist that people who need your approval to act go through many other levels of the hierarchy first — it doesn't matter in which direction. The point is to slow them down, because you don't want radical changes. A variant is to have departments challenge and criticize each other's proposals and then just pick the winner, thereby guaranteeing they'll never collaborate on anything again.
- If you don't want innovation, high performance, and quality, then withhold praise, express criticism freely, and instill job insecurity. That keeps people on their toes. How else would they know that you have standards? With all due respect — I know he's written a book and he's mellowed, but he's retired now — I used to call this the Harold Geneen macho school of management. It said that people do their best work when terrified. If you don't have strong standards, they just won't perform.
- Change policies in secret and reorganize unexpectedly and often. If you don't want people taking initiative to solve problems, then you must keep them in suspended animation, never knowing when another directive from corporate is going to cut things to ribbons again. Some of our old-style manufacturing plants found that the best way to close the facility was to announce it on the radio that morning as people were driving to work. That way, they didn't lose productivity and they avoided anxiety that might slow things down.
- Be control conscious. Count everything that can be counted as often as possible. If you don't want people to take initiatives and solve problems, you want to have more measurements than you need. You want to measure so much that all behavior will go only to the measures. To stamp out

11

initiative, make sure there is no spare change that people could ever invest in a special project that's not in a budget somewhere. Make sure that so much time is taken up just meeting the measures that nobody would be able to think about investing in the future or solving a problem.

- The attitude at the top should be, "We already know everything important there is to know about this business. We've been in business a long time, and we've been successful, so we'll just keep doing what we've been doing."

A good place to start in changing the culture is to reverse the old rules.

Increase receptivity to and forums for new ideas. Many companies are already doing this through quality processes. What about other processes? How many people are reached? What about ideas for things that can't be done right the first time because they've never been done before? That is one of the slight contradictions in "Do it right the first time." You have to have done it once before to know what right is. Make sure those kinds of quality standards aren't a barrier to experimentation and to trying new things.

Faster approval and less red tape are required. Do things really have to go through so many levels of signatures?

Increase praise, recognition for achievements, and open communication — especially advance warning of changes in plans.

Maintain an attitude that you're always learning and can learn from any source. This helps convert change from being a threat to being an opportunity.

Change is always a threat when it's done to me or imposed on me, like it or not. But it's an opportunity if it's done by me. It's my chance to contribute and be recognized. That's the simple key to all of this: Make it an opportunity for people and reward them for it. Throughout every rank of American organizations, we must think about problem solving as entrepreneurs do. They think of every problem as an opportunity to do it better. This is the kind of attitude we need.

The Corrective Action Approach to Improving Quality and Productivity

In today's fast-paced and highly competitive marketplace organizations are under pressure on all fronts to remain viable and profitable, but there are two key factors that can determine whether they can pull out in front of the race or fall behind — *quality* and *productivity.* The quality of your organization's services and products will determine whether the market will continue to demand them or increase its demand. Productivity will determine whether your organization will reap a profit or loss in the provision of its services and products. While neither quality nor productivity account for the whole picture with regard to market demand and profitability, they can and do have a major impact, but more importantly they are factors that can be controlled by managers and employees at all levels of the organization. Thus, the ability to identify and solve quality and productivity problems is critical to organizational performance and success.

This book is designed to provide readers with a variety of techniques to improve their organization's ability to solve quality and productivity problems. We present both sides of the problem-solving process: the analytic techniques you will use, and methods for organizing, managing, and participating in the process. Regardless of the merit of any analytic technique, it will prove less than effective if those who are using it to do not understand the people and organizational side of implementation. With this in mind, we have devoted the last two parts of the book to the issue of managing and organizing the problem-solving process.

The analytic techniques and methods of managing the process are applicable in any industry from manufacturing to services and in any department from production to personnel, as well as in government and nonprofit sectors. The problem-solving process presented here is based on Goodmeasure's work helping a wide variety of organizations with productivity and quality problems. We have found the process to be quite effective. While the book is aimed primarily at managers, individual contributors and employees may also find the techniques and methods useful in their work.

There are four parts in the book, each serving a different purpose. In the first part, *Definitions and Overview,* we present an introduction to the key basic concepts and to the relationship between Corrective Action and Productivity and Quality of Work Life Approaches.

In the second part, *The Five-Step Process,* we present the five analytic steps which comprise the Corrective Action Process. In the first step, quality and productivity problems are identified. In the second step, the problems are classified and prioritized. In the third step, assignments are made to work on the problem. The analytic techniques for problem solving are presented in the fourth step. The last step is devoted to implementing the solutions that have been developed.

In the third part, *Getting Organized for Action,* we present the concept of a problem-solving team and techniques for establishing and organizing such teams. In addition, this part of the book provides guidelines for participating effectively in teams, conducting meetings and discussions, and choosing and "selling" projects and recommendations.

The last part, *Managing Teams,* provides guidelines and an approach for managers who are undertaking a quality or productivity improvement program. In *Managing Teams* we explore a wide range of issues relevant to managers from the role and responsibilities of managers with regard to the Corrective Action Process and problem-solving teams to how to create an organizational environment which is supportive of high quality and productivity and of high organizational effectiveness. In this part we also discuss the critical role of a steering committee to guide and support Corrective Action and the Quality or Productivity Improvement Process and to ensure that these processes are integrated into the system.

As you will see, the book has been designed to maximize its usefulness to managers. Thus, in addition to providing readers with chapters that describe the approach in detail, we also have included a number of short summaries of key points, guidelines, forms for planning, and checklists.

Basic Concepts and Definitions

Quality

Quality means meeting standards for excellence in your product or service — whether your product is the pieces of equipment your company sells; reports, analyses, training programs, marketing plans, sales calls; or any of the numerous other tangible or intangible "things" organizational units produce.

Throughout this book the term "customer" is used to represent all of the various users of the output of your area. So the *idea of quality* is not confined to the organization's core product or service (widgets for a widget maker, classroom teaching for a school, monetary transactions for a bank), but the concept of quality is applicable to *every* department or area within any part of any organization — because all of them "produce" something for someone else's use. Being aware of who is using your work and for what purposes can be an important first step in improving quality.

Productivity

Productivity refers to the amount of work turned out in a given amount of time: output per labor hour. It is the efficiency measure that looks at whether the organization uses its resources wisely and therefore brings in surplus revenues at the level the organization needs, whether it is a profit-making enterprise or a nonprofit organization.

Productivity is not simply a mechanical matter of turning out the work faster, because then quality sometimes suffers. Instead, it is often a matter of "working smarter, not harder," as the current saying goes.

In this book we consider problem-solving techniques and modes of organization for implementing solutions that apply to *productivity improvement* — getting more output — as well as to *quality improvement* — getting better, defect-free output. The ways of treating, motivating, and mobilizing people for "working smarter" are useful for both goals.

Problem Solving and Corrective Action

Once standards for quality and productivity are set based on "customer" or user needs and requirements, and organization revenue objectives, an organization can begin to examine and remove the roadblocks that cause defects, lower quality, and limit productivity. That is the essence of problem solving toward *corrective action:* to correct the things that stand in the way of high quality and productivity, to "fix" the problem-causers, and to solve the underlying causes of inadequate performance.

Problem solving and corrective action are not fire fighting. Instead of merely putting out the fire, a good Corrective Action Process will find the causes of the blaze and try to remove them so that future fires are prevented. Thus, effective problem solving requires tools and skills beyond the obvious ones of throwing water on the flames. It requires the ability to get to the underlying causes so the right problems are addressed, to set priorities about which issues to tackle first, to get the right people working on them, to apply careful analyses to the factors involved, and to guarantee implementation of solutions.

In this book problem solving is broken down into five steps, and comprehensive guidelines are provided for each step. This is designed to ensure that corrective action lives up to its definition — that the actions taken are indeed "corrective" so that a particular problem never recurs.

Teams

Teams are groups of people working together collaboratively toward common ends. As such, they are a cornerstone of *quality and productivity improvement.* In a certain sense, an organization dedicated to high levels of quality and productivity has to function as a large team in that activities across areas need to be coordinated, departments and functions need to work collaboratively, and everyone needs to feel ownership of goals larger than those of his or her own area. Teamwork does *not* mean everyone doing the identical thing side-by-side or making all decisions together; it does mean sharing the responsibility for a common task or problem. Thus, more teamwork is a desirable overall objective for a high quality and productivity organization.

Beyond this, teams are used specifically to solve particular problems interfering with high quality and productivity. There are many circumstances (outlined later in the section *Assignment of Responsibility*) when teams rather than individuals are the best vehicle for corrective action, because team formation ensures shared responsibility, a diversity of talents and perspectives, and commitment to implementation.

Working in and through teams requires special skills on the part of both team members and those managing the team. Actions involving team participation must be carefully managed to get the best results. A great deal of space in this book is devoted to understanding how to form and manage problem-solving teams.

Critical Success Factors

The foundation for the success of quality and productivity improvement is an organization with a climate or culture conducive to high performance — motivating to its people, informed as to its performance, and open to suggestions for change. Thus, critical success factors are those aspects of an organization's culture (its messages about what kinds of behavior are appropriate) and structure (its patterning of relationships and allocation of responsibilities) that reinforce a dedication to quality and productivity.

In addition to correcting particular problems that cause lowered productivity or poor quality, every organizational unit should also be examining its basic culture and structure to see if the foundation for continuing quality and productivity is there — to see if problems can be anticipated and prevented as well as solved, and to see if new ideas for innovations and improvements can be developed or used. Critical success factors involve those underlying organizational conditions that make a difference in ultimate and long-term results.

This book goes much further than the usual "productivity improvement programs" or "quality campaigns" in calling attention to building a total environment receptive to *continuing* problem solving and *continuing* improvement.

Corrective Action and P/QWL Approaches

Quality of Work Life in Context
(Barry A. Stein)

Introduction

In the last 20 years or so a great deal of theoretical and practical work has been done on the possibility of developing more humanistic work places. This activity has also included an enormous amount of experimentation, both in the social psychological or laboratory sense, and in the form of actual change projects introduced into organizations. Experiments have taken place in the United States and in dozens of other countries, in large and small organizations of all sorts, and in centrally planned as well as market economies. Nevertheless, it remains unclear what conclusions can be drawn. In some ways, the more that is learned, the more caution is needed in making predictions.

There is, plainly, much more to be done. However, the strong forces driving this experimentation show just how important the answers are. These forces can be clustered into two categories. One is change in national and international economic environments, characterized by increasing scarcity of critical resources, growing interdependence of countries and industries, doubts about the benefits of growth, more concern over ecological and environmental issues, greater questioning of the ethics of our present economic distributions, a considerable mistrust of technology and, of course, high inflation. The second category concerns changes in the labor force and in people's orientation toward work, and is characterized by an apparent loss of the traditional work ethic, greater focus on personal rewards and entitlements, a growing sense of individual righteousness, younger and increasingly better educated workers, and labor force growth by incorporation of relatively nontraditional workers, including, but not limited to, women.

An equally sweeping generalization about the results of these forces is this: The former (environmental change) produces a relatively stagnant economy, with costs increasing faster than benefits. The latter (change in the labor force) produces increasingly dissatisfied workers, including managers and professionals, competing for a scarce resource — good jobs.

The issue is not whether productivity and a high quality of work life (QWL) go together; that is too global (Figure 1.1). The issue is to define the circumstances in which they can be jointly increased. To that end, I offer a framework for action and a description (checklist) of what helps. There are no guarantees, of course, but we can increase the probability of success, and options must be viewed in that light.

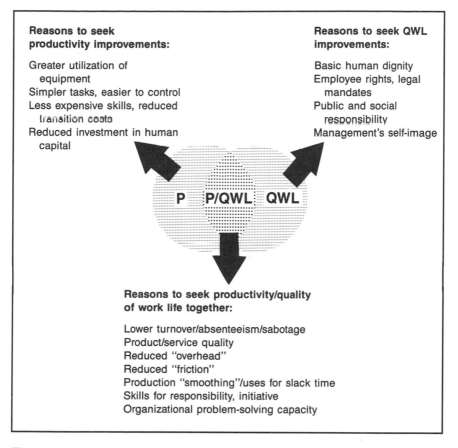

Reasons to seek productivity improvements:

Greater utilization of
    equipment
Simpler tasks, easier to control
Less expensive skills, reduced
    transition costs
Reduced investment in human
    capital

Reasons to seek QWL improvements:

Basic human dignity
Employee rights, legal
    mandates
Public and social
    responsibility
Management's self-image

P   P/QWL   QWL

Reasons to seek productivity/quality of work life together:

Lower turnover/absenteeism/sabotage
Product/service quality
Reduced "overhead"
Reduced "friction"
Production "smoothing"/uses for slack time
Skills for responsibility, initiative
Organizational problem-solving capacity

Figure 1.1 Reasons for Undertaking P/QWL

Background Considerations

Let's start with productivity. No elaborate definitions are necessary. What we mean by productivity is just how much of a specific product can be generated from a given set of resources. Simply, how much is produced from a given stock of equipment, money, and people. This definition says nothing about direction. It doesn't at all ensure, even if productivity is high, that the things being produced are the things we really want. This sort of productivity merely measures the mechanical efficiency of a system.

We should distinguish efficiency and effectiveness. As Peter Drucker defines it, efficiency is "doing things right." Effectiveness is "doing the right thing," and for that we need different objectives and measures. One such objective — one that is internal to the organization — is QWL because we can appropriately think of the task of organizations as the satisfaction of needs, both for customers or social units and for workers or employees.

Traditionally, much of the attention to productivity has been related to capital equipment, new technology, or facilities; in short, to those things that multiply human effort. But I'd like to draw attention instead to "people productivity" or "worker productivity" or "employee productivity." (The phrase "labor productivity" has been preempted by economists to signify that multiplier effect.) If we look at the people side, we can see that there is nothing automatic about those multiplicative effects. The mere availability of tools does not guarantee productivity, effectiveness, or even use. For example, the easiest way to stop an organization dead in its tracks is for everyone to do *precisely* what they're told — no less, but also no more. Because instructions are necessarily incomplete, organizations expect their members to put things in context, to decide what is really entailed in an instruction, and to decide how to achieve the *objective* rather than merely to follow the order.

As organizations have become more complex, more technically sophisticated, and more subject to changing environmental pressures, we require even more worker collaboration at all levels. We need them to *think* about their activities. For the same reasons, it is increasingly impossible by any means of observation to know whether people are actually doing what they need to do to be most effective. We depend, in the final analysis, on people's thoughtful and deliberate willingness to participate.

Productivity of people requires four major conditions:

1. Motivation — wanting to act effectively and to use available resources. People need to be motivated to be productive.
2. Knowledge — even with motivation, what can be done? What should be useful? What are the unmet objectives, untapped opportunities, or unsolved problems? And how should one begin?
3. Actual Capacity — people need *to be able* to do those things. It's not adequate simply to have ideas and direction, and to be motivated. It takes tools, resources, support, and legitimacy.
4. Integration — coordination and management. Otherwise, individual efforts do not produce *organizational* results. They might be irrelevant to each other, may even conflict, but certainly do not build on and reinforce each other. At best, the result is a suboptimized system.

It is also important to differentiate long-term from short-term effects. In general, organizations are much less effective than they could be, in part because of unused latent resources. Many or most people do not work to the limits of their capacity or even their interest. Some of that latent capacity is fairly easy to see. For example, as every study or analysis shows without fail, every organization has in it people with good (but unused) ideas or skills. In principle, it is possible to tap those resources directly. That's the short-term component of productivity.

However, there is a more critical issue concerning systematic human resource development over time, whether that involves training, career planning, reward systems, or organizational redesign. Attempts to increase productivity and QWL often flounder because of the notion that the issues are short term only, and that QWL can simply be "installed" as a new data process system is installed. Moreover, it is almost always possible to increase short-term productivity at the expense of the long-term — an organizational equivalent to winning the battle but losing the war. And because of most organizational reward systems, this is regrettably common.

QWL is a more complex notion, and one about which there is less clear agreement. Let me identify six key components:

1. Control or Autonomy — the capacity to affect one's own environment. Whatever the details, some notion of reasonable freedom of action at work is inseparable from the broad concept of QWL.
2. Recognition — being known as an individual; being visible not only personally, but also as a contributor.
3. Belonging — being part of a social unit. Recognition addresses the need to be distinguished and differentiated from others; belonging refers to the complementary need to be a part of a group and to have something in common with others.
4. Rewards — benefits that flow from work. Rewards are either internal — a sense of growth, development, challenge, competence, and opportunity; or external — pay, status, position or promotion, and other organizational benefits.
5. Decent Work Conditions — they're often left out because it is easy to forget, when focusing on developmental issues, that a physically decent place of work is also important.
6. Dignity and Respectful Treatment — people are entitled to be treated with dignity under any circumstances, by everyone.

If this is what QWL means, why should we be interested in it? There are several possible answers. Many people value a high QWL, defined in this way, simply because of the belief that people deserve it and that it is good in and of itself. Others see it as something that leads to other desirable things, such as stronger motivation to work, greater productivity, and more effective organizations.

These views are not necessarily in conflict. It *is* intrinsically important to provide people with a high quality of life at work — or elsewhere — to the limit of our capacity, whether or not it makes people more productive. But that doesn't mean that we can't also get greater productivity. We can.

However, there is a long-term and a short-term focus. To address the development of people seriously requires time. Environments that enable people to develop and maintain a high QWL require different things from short-run changes that immediately do something to make people feel better. For example, painting everything, sweeping the floor, cleaning up, or providing a new office certainly improve people's work environment, and these can be done quickly. But they do not necessarily last and they do not address the long-term issue of building and maintaining a high QWL. These two problems are different and need to be looked at in different ways.

The Relationship Between Productivity and Quality of Work Life

Do productivity and QWL necessarily go together? No. Do they ever go together? Yes. Can we make them go together? Yes. QWL and productivity are clearly independent. We can increase QWL without the slightest trouble if we accept a loss in productivity. We can do it, for example, by slowing down assembly lines and providing more amenities. In many ways, work can be made more attractive and rewarding for people, so that work life quality increases, but productivity does not. We can also increase productivity without much impact (or a negative impact) on QWL — e.g., by speeding up the assembly line. The historical development of work organizations shows this clearly.

The central feature of industrial organization has perhaps been the continued division of labor which, though praised by Adam Smith, took a new significance in this century because of Frederick Taylor's theory of scientific management, and the modern assembly line. These devices have systematically increased productivity and simultaneously lost more and more of the characteristics that contribute to a high QWL. Indeed, increasing productivity by those methods guaranteed that QWL would be reduced. Having said that, it does not follow — and in fact is untrue — that each must be dealt with separately. We can deal with them together, as many other examples show (e.g., union/management committees, which are becoming much more common. Skeptics might look at the recent history of General Motors' Tarrytown or Fleetwood assembly plants). Many approaches have shown great value, at least in the short run. Self-managed work groups and flexible working hours, for example, have in a number of instances increased people's perceived QWL and measure of productivity. So it is clearly *possible* to raise both together.

The critical question is: Why don't we always (or even usually) succeed in doing this, even when we try to repeat what has worked before or elsewhere? Why these inconsistencies? The answer is a misunderstanding of organizations and organizational process.

There is the mistaken notion that the essence of QWL and productivity *is* their characteristics; that putting in place certain features or options at work creates the result automatically, as if putting a stove in the kitchen were identical to cooking a meal. Adding "participation" — inviting people to a meeting they've never before attended — is no assurance that QWL will rise. QWL and productivity result, or fail to result, from processes that these procedures or structures *permit* but do not guarantee. This misunderstanding is exacerbated by a problem of measurement. If people can't measure the real results (productivity in many service areas, or QWL in general), they often fall back on measures of the steps taken — counting stoves as an index of food quality, or numbers of people participating as an index of QWL.

There are also mistaken notions that simple cause and effect principles apply and that doing any one thing will always bring about the same result. Organizations and people are extremely complex systems, and we still have much to learn about them. But one thing is extremely clear: Organizational results are highly contingent on a whole set of conditions and characteristics. These *interaction* effects are what determine whether things work or not.

Another mistaken notion is that QWL and productivity are direct or primary results of deliberate action. They are not. Rather, they are secondary outcomes of procedures, processes, and structures in the organization and its environment. We *can* modify and act on some of those parameters and that is what we do ordinarily, but the occurrence of the important outcomes — including QWL and productivity — depend on how those actions we can take interact with other characteristics we can modify only indirectly. This is why the "same" program often does not give the same results. Each such application exists in its own setting in a particular organization, with a specific technology, its own set of traditions, and a unique group of people.

We need to pay more attention to the nature of the setting, the character of the organization, and the people, the technology, and the traditions. By the same token, there are many routes to increasing QWL or productivity. We can observe that although two organizations have an equally high QWL in two different units, they may all consist of different elements, may be there for different reasons, and may have arisen from different actions.

Finally, we make a mistake by confusing the long term with the short. Increasing productivity — or QWL — in the long term, which is the important issue, calls for special strategies. To be most productive in the long run requires less than maximum productivity in the short term, because there must always be a reserve component invested for long-term payoff and therefore accounted as a cost earlier. It is unfortunate that the bulk of significant organizational rewards and sanctions stress the short run; quarterly financial statements and performance appraisals are good illustrations of this. We need to recognize these pressures, resist them, and develop different reward and monitoring systems.

It is plausible to suggest, in fact, that in the long run productivity and QWL are more nearly congruent. The trade-offs suggested earlier are more difficult to maintain over time, as secondary effects become more important. For example, although people can put up with great inconvenience, stress, and disappointment in the short run, they are less tolerant as time goes by. They will either leave (an active response) or adjust their effort to the minimum acceptable level (a passive response). In neither case will the drop in productivity be correctly evaluated, because it is difficult to measure the opportunity cost, that is, the productivity foregone. But it is only too real.

The Context for Productivity and Quality of Work Life

These caveats notwithstanding, we can learn much from past and present experiences. One of the most striking observations is this: Every one of our present "innovations" aimed at increasing QWL is actually old. What is new is the context, and therefore, the net reaction or impact. Virtually every significant idea is old. Union management committees, autonomous work groups, job enrichment, and flexible schedules are old concepts. The history of business organizations suggests that many of these ideas were nearly universal, or at least taken for granted, and that over time they have been systematically stripped away.

This history is well worth rediscovering. Anyone interested in autonomous work groups should read *Dynamic Factors in Industrial Productivity* by Seymour Melman.[1] It describes a British automobile company that until the mid-1950s operated on the "gang" system, with groups as large as 300 people operating more autonomously than present autonomous work groups — and on the shop floor at that. The gang selected its own management, decided how to distribute income, and negotiated with plant management about objectives in quantity and quality. As Melman shows, it was measurably more effective than equivalent production in a conventional hierarchy. Everyone's job was "richer" before Taylor showed us how to partition tasks and labor into the smallest and most routinized pieces possible. Or take flexible schedules: That was the *only* choice in a society where factories were the exception rather than the rule. As those traditions died, and the control shifted to organizations, we began to wonder how to get some of those things back.

Of course, some things are new — critically new — but only in context. We have a different labor force, not because people are different, but because their expectations and educations are different. Technology has also advanced. The political/economic environment has changed tremendously. All of these things bear strongly on the problem of increasing QWL and productivity.

In technology, we have moved from a world in which most tasks were simple and visible to one in which tasks are complex and private. Simple observation was adequate to determine the effectiveness of someone digging a ditch, shoveling coal, or hammering nails. External control was therefore easy. Now, however, no form of observation can really assure that people are doing their job to their capacity. Modern organizations at almost every level require people's commitment and will. We depend on people not merely to take directions, but to interpret them and apply them to particular situations. In a world where people's *commitment* is necessary for productivity itself, QWL issues become critical. We have missed the mark on productivity because too much attention has been directed toward capital equipment, as if effective machinery alone was the answer.

Unfortunately, people sometimes fail to recognize that context counts. It's too easy to discard new ideas as "untried," and therefore, too risky or "faddish." But old ideas are even more easily rejected as "old-fashioned" because of the assumption that if a practice was given up, it probably wasn't working. Finally, managers fall back on this position: "If it was good enough for me, it's good enough for them." We shift from a slavish reliance on the traditional to a slavish avoidance of it. If we understand better how to learn the more accurate lessons from experience, we can make much greater progress.

Lessons to be Learned

What have we learned? First, we've learned that there is a great difference between building a new plant or creating a new unit that involves innovative approaches to QWL and productivity, and modifying procedures or structures in an existing facility. The former is much easier and tends to involve the most innovative mechanisms.[2] But the major need is in existing facilities.

Second, we've learned that it's much easier to get things started and show early signs of success than to maintain that success over time, or diffuse the new arrangements more broadly.[3]

Third, we've learned that nothing works in every case, not even participation, as Mulder has demonstrated in some convincing experiments in Holland.[4] In fact, under some conditions participation is massively dysfunctional. Consider the participation of someone whose knowledge of the subject under discussion is nil, whose group skills are few, and who has neither resources nor authority, yet who is meeting with the more experienced and more knowledgeable people. Is that useful, either for the person or the group? No. Even the best ideas need to be set in an appropriate context.

Fourth, we've learned that innovative projects are extremely easy to destroy: Even a casual cold can turn into terminal pneumonia. One large and prestigious manufacturer, well known for its innovative efforts in QWL, built a new plant that for a time was truly remarkable in the vision it embodied and the positive results that were obtained. One physical element was a room that had been set aside for people in the plant as a place where they could go at any time to talk. A new plant manager who came later noted that space had become short and that it might be better to use the room for office space. Since it didn't seem terribly important, even to the employees, and since space was indeed short, no one really objected. But over the next year or so, through several such small erosions of the original vision, the plant changed. It lost some of its vitality and became more conventional, although at the time it was hardly noted. But these are the small, subtle elements that make a different kind of a culture. Cultures are enormously complex, deeply interwoven of a myriad of small details, all of which reinforce it, help to generate it, and shape its daily reality. Changing anything may, in time, change everything.

The following conclusions can be drawn:

- We need a sharper focus on, and better theories about, interaction effects in complex organizations — how things fit together and reinforce, sidetrack, or undercut our efforts.
- We need to pay more attention to the difference between the short term and the long term, and to develop better measures and indicators of long-term effects.
- It's easier to be a pioneer and be there in the beginning to help start something. It's harder to change it later. (This is even true in such atypical organizational contexts as communes or kibbutzim in Israel. Later generations of people who weren't involved with setting it up tend to be less committed.)
- We need to institute innovations more effectively. Implementation counts; how it is done makes a great difference. We need to set up organizational ratchets, things that lock new procedures and processes into place and prevent them from unwinding as soon as the major effort is withdrawn. It isn't enough to have the right ideas, to apply the right principles, and to say the right things. Change takes time, and resources and transitions are difficult to manage. Poor implementation can destroy the best — and best-laid — plans.
- Both too much isolation and too many open boundaries are destructive. Separate units or plants can become walled off from the rest of the organization, but too *little* protection drains energy and resources prematurely. Some boundaries are needed to support an innovative or different arrangement. Balance is the key.

Systems and Structures

The conclusions outlined previously are all aspects of a systemic view. The critical issues in increasing QWL and productivity concern the nature of organizational systems. Structures, therefore, assume great importance because, at the root, organizational systems are defined by their structures. Structures are the patterns in organizations, their tendencies, grooves, paths, and orienting elements; not merely organization charts, which are but the skeletons of organizations. These patterns can be as large and formal as procedures for manufacturing complex products, and can be embodied in the physical arrangements of the machinery, the design of jobs, or performance appraisal procedures. But they can also be subtle, informal, and local. For example: What norms exist about when people come to work or when they leave? How much flexibility is there about "dropping in" on people? How much are people expected to do whatever needs to be done no matter what their formal role? How are relationships and networks built?

Structure, then, means *all* of the patterns that exist in organizations, including informal ones. These patterns are important because they make some things easier and other things harder. To make structural changes, especially in the long term, we need to be aware of the patterns, take advantage of them, and move with them. Cutting across them should be done only for specific and deliberate reasons, because it's hard, tends not to work, and is likely to generate resistance. We also need to understand the patterns so we can modify them and use them to reinforce other desired activities. Changing structure means changing the patterns. With this in mind, we can start by moving with them, at first deviating little, and later, more dramatically. The process of changing organizational structures, which is essential for any genuine organizational change, is thus a form of judo, using the organization's own momentum to bring change. This is the key to successful implementation: understanding and using structure.

There are quite obviously many different ways to think about structure. However, we believe that Kanter's perspective is the most potent for our purposes.[5] She identified two structural elements — the distributions of opportunity and power — that can directly and usefully be linked to QWL and productivity.

Opportunity means not simply promotion, but challenge, growth and development, and progress. Such opportunity is a property of the organization; it is distributed across positions so that people in certain positions have more or different opportunities from people in other positions. This is important because people whose positions offer opportunity are motivated, confident, active, engaged in work, and, ultimately, more competent. People in positions with little opportunity are unmotivated, doubtful of their abilities, unambitious, passive, and, ultimately, ineffective. People tend to change their behavior systematically when they shift from a position that offers opportunity to one that does not, or vice versa. For organizations to make good use of their people requires that they make opportunity widely available.

Power, to a considerable extent, is also a property of the system. It is not carried by individuals in and of themselves, although personal skills are clearly important in using the power made available through the organization. Organizational power is not simple authority in the formal sense. It is a combination of credibility, access to resources, and the capacity to get things done. It is power in the engineering sense — energy expended over time, a means for getting work done. It's not hard to tell who is powerful. Who would you go to for help? Who really gets things done? Who can be left out of decisions, or bypassed? In this sense, people with the same nominal authority can have very different amounts of real power.

Power is critical for several reasons. First, by definition, it takes power to get the work done and to be effective. Second, power, more than anything else, sets good leaders apart from others. The powerful delegate well; they support their subordinates and can afford to share their power with them. And they can deliver — resources, rewards, opportunities, and contacts. Finally, power is important because people without power — the powerless — become petty bureaucrats. They are controlling, rules-minded, and petty. They protect their turf, and deny subordinates and others any power of their own. Women, in particular, often get stereotyped like that — the bossy woman boss. But it is not really characteristic either of women or bureaucrats; it's an effect of powerlessness. A central issue in organizational structure, therefore, is to increase people's access to power in general.

There is a third important structural element, somewhat different in character. Giving people more access to opportunity and power is necessary but not sufficient. Consistent and coherent incorporation of those elements into the system is also necessary. The mechanisms, policies, and procedures to support and maintain them must also be provided. This is often overlooked, yet we have plenty of evidence as well as theory demonstrating that local changes are all too likely to stay local. Indeed, they will decay over time unless an overall structure exists.

The exact forms of such a framework will differ from organization to organization, but two components will always exist. The first ensures integration of the new orientation — e.g., universal access to opportunity and power — into the ongoing and routine operation of the organization. There must be supportive policies and procedures, rewards that encourage such behavior, and adequate information for all employees. The second component is a set of mechanisms that allows people to take action — organizational legitimacy, so to speak. We have found a "parallel structure" particularly useful, consisting of a representative, system-wide steering committee to which individuals and task forces can submit proposals and within which they can explore new options legitimately. Stein and Kanter in their article "Building the Parallel Organization: Permanent Quality of Work Life" offer a full description and case study.[6]

What does this framework do? First, it provides the means to empower the people who are supposed to carry out changes. Second, it makes the management and coordination of the specific efforts and tasks possible. People shouldn't simply do what seems right to *them;* that is often dysfunctional for them and the organization, in the long run if not the short. Their efforts need to be integrated with organizational goals. Third, this framework provides learning, and the capacity for its extensions, application, and diffusion. The ultimate goal is not a few local changes or modified procedures, but a shift in the way the organization operates and uses its people. Fourth, such a framework provides a base for consistent rewards and recognition of those involved as well as those who are expected to take advantage and learn from new ideas and changes.

Systems lacking or not understanding such a framework conduct experiments that lead nowhere and involve people who are not sufficiently recognized and valued. The activities may be interesting, perhaps even *theoretically* relevant and important, but if they're not connected to the overall system, they eventually become like museum pieces, watched from outside, but not perceived as relevant.

These three elements of structure are directly related to the criteria for establishing a high QWL and increasing productivity. Table 1.1 summarizes the criteria for productivity, and shows their relationship to these structural elements. Table 1.2 is a similar display for QWL.

Condition		Derived from
Motivation	Wanting to act	Opportunity
Capacity	Being able to act	Power and opportunity
Knowledge	Knowing how to act	Power
Coordination	Acting together	Framework

Table 1.1 Conditions for Productivity

Condition	Derived from
Autonomy **Control**	Power
Recognition **Visibility**	Power and opportunity
Belonging **Shared Goals**	Power, opportunity, and operating framework
Rewards **Internal/External**	Power, opportunity, and operating framework
Dignity **Respect**	A humane society
Decent Working Conditions	A humane society

Table 1.2 Conditions for High QWL

Productivity first requires motivation. Motivation is strongly influenced by opportunity — whether or not there are adequate challenges and chances for growth and development. Capacity, by definition, is power — access to necessary tools and resources. Knowledge is related to both opportunity and power: opportunity, because access to training and education is itself a part of growth and development; and power, because both that kind of knowledge and knowledge about the organization — its needs, its characteristics, and its condition — are in themselves resources and are empowering. Finally, coordination derives from a connection to an integrating and guiding system, the operating framework.

The conditions for a high QWL are similarly related. One element of power is autonomy or control — the legitimate ability to take the steps needed for the task. Recognition and visibility are related to both opportunity and power because a part of giving opportunity is recognizing those who take advantage of it, and because power is derived in part from visibility and a sense of being known as an individual. The condition of belonging, of having a sense of shared goals, is at once empowering (through relationships with others), opportunity enhancing (through greater understanding and knowledge of organizational needs and goals, and perceptions of personal value), and related to the operating framework (by making explicit and implanting those structures that build and sustain the rewarding of organizational goals and objectives). Similarly, rewards partake of all three structural elements. The last two, dignity or respect and decent work conditions, are enhanced by the structures noted but actually precede them. In a civilized society, there should be no need for discussion about either their importance or appropriateness.

These notions of the importance of structures and of particular structural elements, along with conclusions reached from extensive study of experiences to date, can help launch change projects that can more reliably increase productivity while enhancing QWL. No one and no theory can guarantee success; too much depends on complex choices, situations, and decisions, and results that cannot ever be foreseen. But we can act to increase the probability of successful outcomes.

There is also what Hirschman called the principle of the hiding hand.[7] Successful development projects involve confronting and *resolving* a series of unexpected problems. But had those problems been seen clearly in advance, they would have seemed too risky and most projects would never have been launched. Therefore, everything possible should be done to avoid known traps and promote success, and a system should be created that is fully capable of addressing and solving problems as they arise, rather than assuming that a good start is all that is needed.

All of these principles and conclusions can be summed up in a series of conditions or criteria that need to be met if QWL and productivity are to be increased jointly. To the extent they are met, the probability of successful outcomes will be higher. Since there are three different focuses of action in any project, there are three different but related lists. Table 1.3 lists conditions for the organizational system overall, Table 1.4 concerns the project itself, and Table 1.5 is specifically relevant to the participants.

Outside people have access. People need to obtain information about projects. Otherwise they feel (and are) excluded, and become unsupportive and eventually destructive. This also lays the groundwork for diffusion and extension.

Managers of participants are educated, empowered, and provided with new opportunity. This is the group that is often excluded and even undercut. Yet their support is necessary and can easily be gained by applying exactly the same principles.

Separate management structure exists. It is difficult or impossible to manage an innovative project with a structure set up to manage entirely different activities. A separate or parallel structure more appropriate in scope is needed.

Program is ongoing. Progress is the key: People become accustomed to any new state. The essence is *continuing* access to new opportunities and challenges.

No free lunches: work gets done. It is essential to keep doing whatever is the normal work. Anyone can feel better and do new things if they are relieved of their normal responsibilities. However, people can almost always do more if they wish to, and if they have the tools.

Table 1.3 System Checklist

Means are consistent with ends. The project has to operate according to its goals. If participation is an objective, people cannot simply be ordered to do a project. The first tests are the hardest and the most important. Build opportunity and power into the essence of the project itself.

Actions are legitimate. There must be adequate support and authority to allow actions in the project to be seen as legitimate and accountable. People sometimes do more than they are technically allowed, but it is less effective and there is often backlash.

Tasks are relevant. Specific issues being addressed by or within the project need to be important for the system. There is no point in launching a change project that deals with trivial or back-burner tasks; no one will care.

Programs, objectives, and tasks are clear. Good plans and well worked out programs are important. People (inside and outside) should know exactly what they are trying to do and why. Fishing expeditions and wishful thinking have no place in projects.

Measures and milestones exist. There should be standards by which people can evaluate progress and processes to change direction if necessary. These should be both short term and long term in nature.

Early results are sought. Don't ask people to wait five years before any results will be visible. People involved need a sense of progress to continue their commitment, and people outside will lose interest even more rapidly.

Table 1.4 Project Checklist

Those affected are represented. This principle is as important in organization change as it was in the American Revolution. Take it seriously.

Set a standard of "informed choice." People need to be able to choose their own rate and level of involvement (or not) after adequate information and understanding. The process of educating people is useful in itself, and without it, no choice can be trusted.

Variety of opportunities exist. Do not expect or ask all people to get involved in any one way. Provide a range of alternatives. Ask what would be a significant opportunity and give people some choices. And don't be upset by a small start; it's better than a total rejection.

Access exists for resources, information, training. People need support and tools if their efforts are to be effective. This also means that time must be allowed for learning and "getting up to speed." An investment in learning time now will pay off later.

People are rewarded and recognized. This should not be a "spare time" effort to be put aside when "real work" is to be done. Equally formal and serious attention needs to be paid to people's performance on projects. If recognition is not the norm, create a new norm.

A Few Don'ts

Don't punish people for not participating.

Don't create opposing teams. If several projects are involved, or if several different activities go on under the same project umbrella, make sure they don't seem to be competing. No one has to be best.

Don't think of "either/or" results. Just as problems cannot be entirely foreseen, neither can benefits. The end result may be very different from anything expected, yet a splendid contribution. It's easy to think that if the result is unexpected, it's worthless.

Table 1.5 Participants' Checklist

We have learned much in the last few years. Those who are disenchanted with past experience, or who do not believe in the possibility of generating viable new organizations with high productivity and QWL, are thinking in terms of the wrong models — simple causality rather than complex interaction. The tools to accomplish effective organizational change are within our grasp. And we are beginning to round out the understanding needed to use them.

References

1. Melman, S. *Dynamic Factors in Industrial Productivity.* London: Blackwell, 1956.
2. Lawler, E. E. "New Plant Revolution." *Organization Dynamics* 6, No. 3, 1978.
3. Walton, R. "The Diffusion of New Work Structures: Explaining Why Success Didn't Take." *Organizational Dynamics* 3, No. 3 (1975): 2-22.
4. Milder, Mauk. "Power Equalization Through Participation?" *Administrative Science Quarterly,* March 1971.
5. Kanter, R. M. *Men and Women of the Corporation.* New York: Basic, 1977.
6. Stein, B. A., and R. M. Kanter. "Building the Parallel Organization: Permanent Quality of Work Life." *Journal of Applied Behavioral Sciences,* Fall 1980.
7. Hirschman, A. O. *Development Projects Observed.* Washington, DC: The Brookings Institution, 1967.

PART TWO
THE FIVE-STEP PROCESS

Introduction

An Overview of the Five-Step Corrective Action Process

In this section the Corrective Action Process will be presented as a series of analytic tasks. The first two steps address the various ways managers can become organized to undertake a Corrective Action Process in their organizations. But regardless of whether corrective action is undertaken by a single individual, a team in one isolated division, or a corporate-wide effort involving hundreds of teams, all will follow the same set of analytic tasks. These are:

Step 1 — Problem Identification
The first step in any problem-solving process is always to identify the problem or problems. Identifying the "customers" of your services and/or products and discovering their requirements is an excellent way to learn about existing or impending problems.

Step 2 — Problem Classification
Once the full gamut of problems has been identified, the next task is to decide which are the most important and which should be addressed sooner rather than later. Pareto analysis is a useful technique for making this determination.

Step 3 — Assignment of Responsibility
Having made the determination about which problem or problems to tackle first, the next task becomes one of assigning an individual or group the responsibility for solving the problem and developing recommendations. Managers should read Parts Three and Four of this book for more about alternative ways of organizing and managing the Corrective Action Process and any teams that may be established.

Step 4 — Application of Problem-Solving Techniques
A variety of problem-solving techniques can be used by individuals or teams to resolve the problems they have been assigned. These include using checklists and graphic illustration of data, process analysis, cause and effect diagrams, force field analysis, and Pareto analysis.

Step 5 — Implementation
Once a recommendation has been accepted the final step is to implement that recommendation.

The Five Steps

Step 1 — Problem Identification

The Corrective Action Process begins with the identification of problems. It is often assumed that everyone already knows what the problems are that keep us from doing our work well. The success really depends on the effectiveness of problem identification — the process of finding the right problems on which to work.

There are three major methods that will help you identify problems. These are:

1. Measuring
   - Collecting and analyzing data.
   - Defining measurements that you will use as standards and then monitoring for conformance against them.
   - Assessing the cost of quality and productivity problems.
2. Asking
   - Soliciting feedback from your customers (internal and external) to find out whether your products or services meet their requirements.
   - Encouraging your own people to identify problems that get in the way of defect-free work.
3. Listening
   - Watching out for signals from your work area.
   - Treating complaints seriously and as important information that will help you manage.
   - Being open to suggestions, especially from unexpected sources.
   - Taking the time to listen without reacting too quickly.

The following are some examples for getting input that will help you to identify the important problems: *Listen to the signals* from every source (measurements, reviews on product life cycle, and, of course, customer complaints). Customer complaints should be taken seriously, even when the complaint appears to be trivial. What appears to be trivial to you may not be trivial to them. Try to reach out to your customers and *find out whether or not your products or services are meeting customer requirements.* Do this regularly since their requirements may change.

There are many tools available to help you in identifying problems. All of these are important ways of collecting information about problems and potential problems.

- Measurements
- Regular reviews
- Customer conversations
- Customer complaints
- Customer surveys
- "Market" feedback and data
- Information about competitors' action

- Regular staff meetings
- Brainstorming sessions
- Cross-level listening sessions

Using Input from your Customers for Problem Identification

In a large complex organization each of us has many customers of many different kinds. One of the major keys to being effective in identifying quality and productivity problems is to maintain close communication with your customers about their requirements. This involves two steps:

1. Awareness of *all* of your customers
   - Who they are
   - What their requirements are
2. Close communication with them about their requirements
   - Adjust expectations
   - Balance all of their requirements

The first task then in problem identification is to identify all of your customers. What is a "customer"? A customer is the *next* person to whom you *directly* supply a product, service, or information. This includes a wide variety of types of customers and kinds of relationships you may have with them, such as the following:

- Sequential or one-way relationships
- Reciprocal relationships
- External to your organization or work area
- Internal to your organization or work area
- Many choices
- Fewer choices
- Long-term contracts
- Short-term contracts
- Long-term importance
- Short-term importance

Understanding these differences can help you identify more customers and better meet their requirements. A *sequential* or *one-way* relationship with a customer is "conventional." You make, and they buy. It's easy to see them as customers.

A *reciprocal relationship* with a customer means that you supply them, and they supply you. They depend on you for some things and you depend on them for other things, like members of a project team, or a manager and subordinates. We sometimes forget these kinds of customers.

Customers who are *external* to your organization or work area don't have to care how well the organization does; they just want the product or service you supply to be done to their requirements. Nothing else matters.

Customers who are *internal* to your organization or work area are those who share your fate as part of the same organization and may have friendships or a history of working with you. This can sometimes make us forget that they are customers. We sometimes believe that our internal customers *must* support us and use our products or services no matter what. But this attitude lowers ultimate effectiveness with the external customer.

Some customers have *many choices* and can take their business elsewhere. There are many competitors out there eager to get their business. We can easily notice the "power" of these customers.

Some customers have *fewer choices* because they depend on us in other ways or feel they have to please us. They can't easily complain about our failure to meet their requirements. They can't easily or quickly move to other suppliers. Your secretary or your employees are good examples. They might have to be provoked a lot before they'd complain or move. Because we have a lot of "power" over these customers, we sometimes forget that these are customers too (whom we supply with information and a work environment), and we fail — to our ultimate regret because we need them — to satisfy *their* requirements.

With some customers we have *long-term contracts*. It's easy to get lulled into a false sense of security with these customers, because there is the feeling that there will be time to make up for mistakes.

With some customers we have *one-shot chances*. We'd *better* get it right the first time or lose their business. They might be a new customer or someone just testing us or a potential future customer. Learning to do it right the first time with long-standing customers helps us when we encounter the one-shot all-or-nothing customer because our quality is guaranteed to be high *always*.

Some customers' importance is *long term*. It doesn't show up right away if we fail to meet their requirements. We may believe we can get away with neglecting them for awhile. (Maybe we won't even be in the same job by the time the quality problem surfaces.) This works against the success of the company of course, which is what we need for our own success. And these are usually the most important customers anyway.

Some customers' importance is *short term*. They might affect your immediate comfort or career — for example, our bosses. But looking out for our careers or pleasing the boss or putting out today's fire can mean neglecting the longer term or more subtle quality requirements important to other customers.

In a large, complex organization — unlike an owner-run corner hot dog stand — each of us has many customers of many different kinds. These customers don't always want exactly the same thing from us or pull us in the same direction. Thus, it is important to know who all your customers are and what their requirements are. Communication about requirements should not be a one-shot endeavor, but should continue on a regular basis. In other words, customer communication about requirements should become part of your routine way of operating.

_____ **Measurements**
Internal data on the state of the product or service —
its quality, the speed or efficiency with which it is produced, its cost or profitability.

_____ **Regular Reviews**
Meetings with higher officials about your area's work
or periodic assessments of the entire state of the area.

_____ **Customer Conversations**
Informal discussions with users or clients about their
needs and satisfaction/dissatisfaction with what you
supply them.

_____ **Customer Complaints**
Customer-initiated expressions of grievance; these are
important data, especially in the patterns.

_____ **Customer Surveys**
Formal gathering of data from customers using the
same questions to each customer.

_____ **"Market" Feedback and Data**
Product or service performance in the marketplace,
e.g., ratings against other product.

_____ **Information About the Actions of "Competitors"**
Data about what "competitors" are doing to meet the
needs of the same set of customers you supply.

_____ **Regular Staff Meetings**
Meetings of everyone reporting directly to a single
manager in which information is exchanged which
helps people see their subarea in relation to the whole
area.

_____ **Brainstorming Sessions**
Formal meetings designed to elicit agendas for
problem-solving or productivity/quality improvement.

_____ **Cross-Level Listening Sessions**
Opportunities for employees across several levels to
discuss their work as they see it, with the manager
simply listening for issues, problems, or opportunities.

Checklist: Tools for Identifying Problems

Invite employees to discuss concerns or problems that may interfere with productivity or quality before there is a major disaster. Make clear that you want early warnings, no matter how trivial they may seem . . . and don't make people feel foolish for mentioning them.

Hold regular "office hours" in which you welcome employee visits to discuss work-related concerns or anything on their mind that bears on productivity and quality.

Be open-minded and questioning.

Don't jump to conclusions about the source of problems. Probe, ask questions, explore options, and look for more data.

Allow employees to ramble. Don't insist on a well-defined problem statement. Often letting them talk gives you more insight into what is *really* going on than the initial statement of "what's the matter."

Thank people for bringing problems to your attention. Make it easy for them to discuss bad news, and don't shoot the messenger who brings it.

Make it legitimate to discuss problems by bringing them up yourself, especially ones in which you have some responsibility. Don't create myths that "everything is wonderful"; admit that things can always be improved.

Guidelines: Helping Employees Discuss Work-Related Problems

Step 2 — Problem Classification

The second step in the Corrective Action Process is the classification and prioritization of problems. After first identifying what the important problems are, you must be able to group them and pull out the ones you want to solve first. In the course of doing this you will be broadening and deepening your perspective on the problem, and getting angles on it that may help you solve it.

One of the most useful tools for prioritizing and classifying problems is known as the *Pareto Principle.* It is a simple technique to identify what problems should be tackled first. Most of the time a few categories will account for a large percentage of the total problems. A few problems will account for a large percentage of the total cost of poor quality and low productivity. This is the rule of the vital few and the trivial many.

Vilfredo Pareto was an Italian engineer turned economist who studied the distribution of individual income in Italy. He demonstrated that a large part of the wealth tends to be held by a small percentage of the population. W. Edwards Deming, the American father of Japanese quality circles, showed that the same relationship holds for quality control. The Pareto Principle is simply a means of identifying the few problems whose solutions will bring the greatest rewards. It is more economical to focus on the vital few problems that bring major results, instead of the trivial many that provide minor results.

Figure 2.1 shows a Deming-based example of a Pareto analysis for a series of accounts at a paper mill. Category A is the vital few, where the shaded region indicates that 60 percent of the total cost of poor quality is associated with this one account. Categories B through G are the trivial many — increasing quality in all of these categories would represent only a 40 percent increase in quality.

In addition to the Pareto analysis there are a number of other indicators that will help you to decide which problems fall into the category of the "vital few" and deserve primary attention. You should use the checklist of priority indicators whenever possible to determine the most important problems in your work area. It is well worth your time to analyze each problem in terms of the nine indicators: history, clarity, extent, visibility, complexity, strength of concerns, agreement and support, time pressure, and communication and symbolic value. Your analysis and classification of problems will be even stronger when you use the Pareto analysis in conjunction with the nine priority indicators. Higher priorities should be assigned to problems that also rank high on these indicators.

Figure 2.2 shows an example of Pareto analysis applied to a problem in a marketing and manufacturing organization. A large machine tool company had recently started to market certain upgrading "kits" for its three major product lines, here known as Product A, Product B, and Product C. The kits, however, took more time to sell to customers, as well as to manufacturers, than had originally been expected. The company wondered whether or not to continue producing these items.

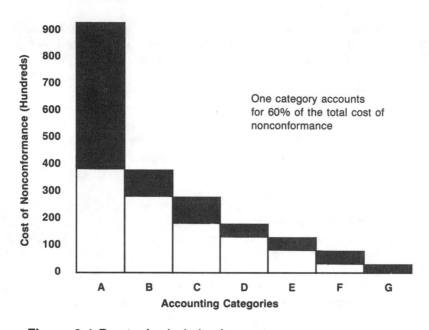

Figure 2.1 Pareto Analysis by Accounts

When Pareto analysis was applied, it turned out that kits for Product A, which comprised only 13 percent of the total orders for kits, provided 66 percent of the sales dollars for kits. On the other hand, the kits that comprised 68 percent of the total orders for the kits produced only 7 percent of the sales dollars for kits.

In many respects the kits presented several difficult problems. Special parts were needed from vendors; they were manufactured in addition to the normal workload, often requiring overtime by the manufacturing staff; and quality control had to develop special testing procedures. In most of the regions, the sales staff found that customers using the kits were extremely satisfied and they were becoming an important marketing tool for the mainline machine tools product. Although most agreed that the kits were important, a solution had to be found to get the kits to customers more quickly and easily. In this case, the problem was analyzed and met not only the "vital few" Pareto Principle, but the criteria for greater extent, complexity, and agreement.

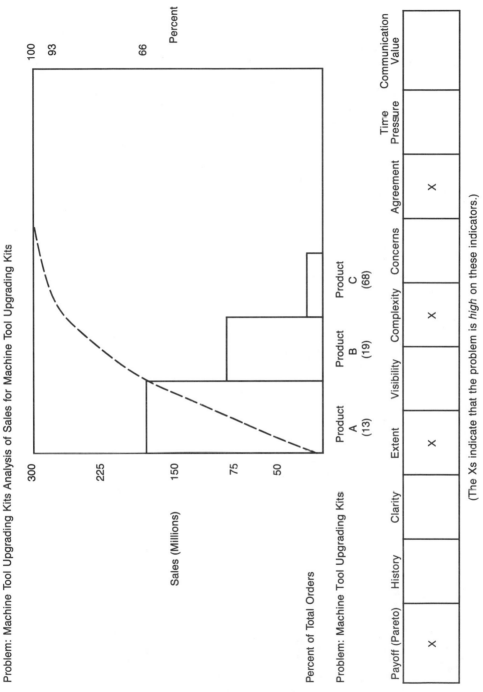

Figure 2.2 Pareto Analysis Applied in a Marketing and Manufacturing Organization

Figure 2.3 shows Pareto analysis applied to the service organization of a copying machine manufacturer. The service department had been receiving complaints from customers for several years, but had paid little attention to these in a systematic fashion. Recently, the complaints were becoming more frequent, and a decision was made to examine the problem thoroughly. The president of the firm had begun to stress the idea of quality and found the increase in complaints to be a source of embarrassment to the firm.

The executive in charge of quality decided to make a "showcase" out of this problem to demonstrate the firm's commitment to improving quality and had little trouble in getting support from the service department to solve the problem. When the managers in the service department analyzed the kinds of complaints they were receiving, it was apparent that the complaints fit the Pareto distribution quite nicely. If they focused on the "vital few" or the complaints about response time, they might solve 54 percent of the problem. In this case, the service problem not only met the Pareto criteria, but had a long history, clarity, visibility, agreement, support and communication, and symbolic value.

Returning to the technique you can use for problem classification, the next step is to list the problems in priority order on the basis of how many categories you have checked (Table 2.1). You may then classify problems on the basis of how quickly you will want to resolve them. For instance, the most important should receive action now; those that are less of a priority should receive attention within the next two months, and the rest should be reviewed after a three-month waiting period (Table 2.2).

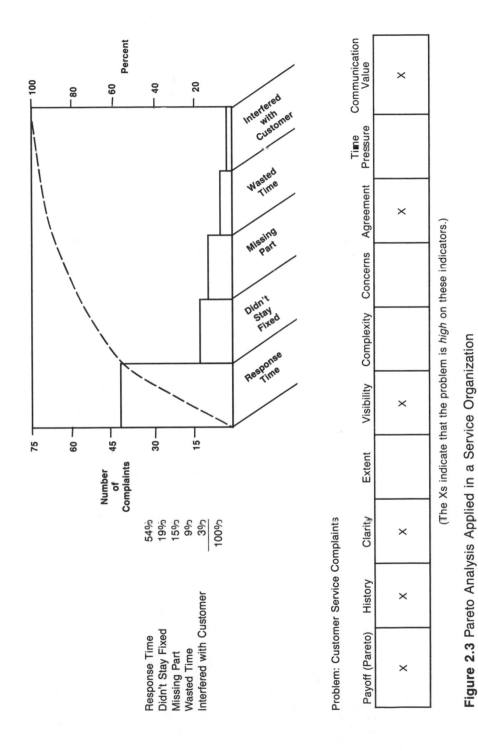

Problem: Customer Service Complaints

	Percent

Response Time — 54%
Didn't Stay Fixed — 19%
Missing Part — 15%
Wasted Time — 9%
Interfered with Customer — 3%
100%

Problem: Customer Service Complaints

(The Xs indicate that the problem is *high* on these indicators.)

Figure 2.3 Pareto Analysis Applied in a Service Organization

For each problem, check the box if it is *high* on the measure. The problems with many checks should be tackled first.

Problem:	Payoff (Pareto)	History	Clarity	Extent	Visibility	Complexity	Concerns	Agreement	Time Pressure	Communication Value
1.										
2.										
3.										
4.										
5.										
6.										
7.										
8.										
9.										
10.										
11.										
12.										

Table 2.1 Problem Analysis Form
(Copyright © 1983 Goodmeasure, Inc. Cambridge, MA. All rights reserved.)

Relist the Problems in Priority Order

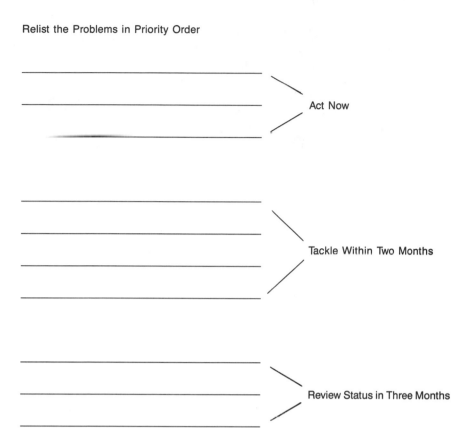

Table 2.2 Problem Priority Order Form

There are three general rules that you should keep in mind when you are try-ing to prioritize problems:

1. It is important to *learn from previous attempts you or others made to solve a particular problem.* Find out some of the history: What was tried and might have failed before? Is the problem defined and stated correctly? Has another department/organization attempted to solve this problem or is there a person or task force already assigned to resolve it? Many problems pop up in different guises at different times; it is important to respond to the right one.

2. Keep in mind that *some problems may be too large and complex to be solved in their entirety.* In this case, it is better to break them down into smaller, manageable chunks, and tackle these as "subproblems." But don't lose sight of connections between them. Sometimes organizations assign pieces of problems to specialists who never get together, and consequently go off in different directions, guaranteeing that the overall problem is never solved.
3. Try to *look for early successes and fast action.* This helps people to feel good about their efforts, to see that the Corrective Action Process does in fact work, and will increase their commitment to maintaining quality and increasing productivity in your organization.

History
How often has this problem come up before? What happened when you tried to resolve it?

Clarity
How clear is the statement of the problem? How concrete is its definition?

Extent
How widespread is it? How many customers does it affect? How many employees identify the same problem?

Visibility
How visible is it? How many customers besides those affected know about it or its consequences?

Complexity
How complex is it? How many kinds of activities are involved in it?

Strength of Concerns
How strong are the concerns of the customers affected by it? How strong are the concerns of the employees identifying the problem?

Agreement and Support
How much agreement is there about the definition of the problem? How much agreement is there about the need for solution? How much willingness is there to implement solutions?

Time Pressure
How urgent is the problem? How immediate are any negative consequences of postponing solution?

Communication and Symbolic Value
Can solving this problem serve as an example? Would it have value to customers/employees as a symbol of commitment to quality?

Checklist: Questions to Use in Determining Problem Priority

Step 3 — Assignment of Responsibility

The third step in the Corrective Action Process is the assignment of responsibility — determining who should take responsibility for solving a problem. As a manager you should be actively involved in deciding who on your staff should solve problems.

The process begins by classifying problems and deciding three issues:

1. How many people should be involved (giving information, expertise, resources)?
2. How many other units may need to be involved and from what parts of your organization?
3. How complex or simple is the problem?

Problems should always be tackled and solved at the lowest possible level in the organization. In many cases it is appropriate to have a problem solved on a one-to-one basis, or perhaps by an existing team. When problems are more complex and affect many people from your own area or more than one area, they should be solved by the formation of problem-solving teams.

There are four options available to you in deciding who should be responsible for solving a problem.

1. Take solitary action as a manager and do it all yourself.
2. Delegate the responsibility to an individual or perhaps an existing team that is already equipped to handle this problem.
3. Form a problem-solving team, either within your area or across work areas.
4. Pass on the problem to another group (higher level or cross-organizational) if the problem cuts across organizational lines.

There are a number of useful guidelines to help you decide where responsibility for solving a problem should be placed. Taking responsibility for solving the problem yourself is most appropriate when these conditions are met:

- There is a clear solution.
- You have an explicit mandate to solve these types of problems.
- You possess more expertise to solve the problem, i.e., the problem calls for someone with specialized knowledge and you have the appropriate background, education, or experience.
- No one else is overly concerned about the problem or would have their own skills enhanced and developed by assisting you. The problem may be uninteresting to others and they wouldn't learn much from working on it.
- The issue is relatively routine, i.e., something you deal with on a regular basis.
- Time constraints are great — quick action is required and you would not have enough time to delegate or put a team together.

- You need to exercise control not only over the results, but ways in which these results are obtained. You may need to direct the implementation of the solution — who is involved, the tasks carried out, the sequence of steps, etc.

If you do decide that managerial action is most appropriate, there are several things you should be prepared to do.

- It is important to act quickly, and not let the issue drag on unresolved because it may damage your credibility, hurt morale, and cost the organization money.
- Others should be notified of the actions you are taking and when you expect to see results because it may affect their work.
- Don't volunteer others in ways that give them little choice about whether or not they really can participate as this creates resistance and you may get people who aren't committed to the problem.
- Whenever possible, do find ways to involve others, especially if it might be helpful to them in their own development.
- This could give them a chance to watch you in action, and learn more about the organization. It also will improve their competence and reflect nicely on you.

In many cases it will be appropriate for you to delegate the problem to an individual or perhaps to a team that is working on a similar problem, or is just finishing up its work. If someone has the problem area as an assignment you certainly won't want to undercut him or her or step on any toes by giving the assignment to a completely new team. When you do delegate, it is important that the problem be given to the lowest possible level in the organization, but still keeping in mind that the person should possess the necessary expertise to resolve it effectively.

The time pressures for resolving the problem should be manageable and not unreasonable — enough to let the person learn and research the issue and create a solution. And while you may have a clear idea of the result you want (solve Problem X by selling 10 more units), you should be able to release control over the means to achieve this result to the individual or team in charge. Let them decide the strategy to pursue for meeting your goal. Finally, the problem should involve low interdependency with other organizations; the actions taken in your area should have little direct impact on another area. You don't want to create problems for another area or make changes unilaterally when you should have used a collaborative process.

In summary, delegation to an individual or existing team is appropriate when the following criteria are met:

- The person or group has clear expertise to solve the problem.
- The person or group already has this area as part of their assigned responsibility.

- The problem can be solved at a lower level.
- Persons under you possess the necessary information and resources to solve the problem.
- Some individual or group shows real interest in tackling this problem.
- A team has previously worked on this or a related problem.
- Your boss or other managers do not expect you personally to solve the problem.
- Time pressures are moderate, but manageable (the more time available the better).
- The outcome and results are clearly specified or known, but the means to achieve these can be decided by someone other than yourself.
- Few or no other departments or organizations are involved (low interdependency).

When you decide to delegate the problem to an individual or an existing team you still have some important responsibilities as a manager. These include defining the ground rules and expectations as well as the limits of the problem — how much will be tackled by this person or team. It is important to be clear about the responsibilities and expectations in advance. You should also leave them alone as much as you can, but monitor the progress regularly: Delegation does not equal abdication. When asked, be ready to serve as a resource. Be sure to give recognition where it is due, whether this is formal or informal. Finally, act quickly in both your decision to accept or reject their recommendations and in implementing them. By acting quickly the problem will be elimated quickly and your subordinates will see that their contributions were useful and valued.

The following are some guidelines you can use when delegating a problem to an individual or team:

- Decide ahead of time how much of the problem can be turned over and communicate this.
- Define the ground rules and expectations. Devise a work plan, set deadlines and checkpoints; decide who will be involved, how much time to spend, etc.
- Review process and results against plan at regular intervals.
- Troubleshoot for them, especially when they need cooperation from another work area or department.
- Monitor the individual or team's progress.
- Reward and recognize the individual or team's work.
- Act quickly in deciding whether to accept recommendations and then act quickly to implement them.
- Inform the rest of the department what is happening.

The third alternative for solving a quality or productivity problem is to form a problem-solving team and let a group of employees assume responsibility for the problem. But as we all know, simply designating a group of people to be a task team does not automatically work. There is still a lot of careful management involved, which starts with deciding *when* teams are appropriate. They are not always the best way. Sometimes doing it yourself or letting a single person do it is better.

Here are some guidelines for when it is appropriate to turn a problem over to a problem-solving team:

- To let others gain expertise or demonstrate their knowledge in solving the problem. If they have experience and ideas, they should be used as resources.
- To build consensus around an issue and let the people who are affected by the problem participate in its resolution. Those who are directly impacted by a problem clearly have a stake in its resolution and undoubtedly will have some ideas about what will and won't work. By involving your people in this way they are more likely to agree about the causes of the problem and the most plausible solution — and probably increase their interest in eliminating the problem, forever.
- To make sure a variety of interests are represented, especially if there may be conflicting points of view. If the problem is especially controversial, there may be divergent views on the causes and solutions all needing to be aired and considered. Otherwise, people who have strong opinions but are left out of the process may not be committed to implementing the solution. Also, you may have missed some important data that someone had to offer.
- To provide an opportunity and enough time to study a problem adequately and come up with the best possible solution. Some problems may have no clear or easy solution and require a longer amount of time to study, analyze, and explore the alternative ways to deal with it. A problem-solving team is a systematic mechanism for examining and resolving particularly difficult problems and legitimately taking the time that is required.
- To allow people to develop their skills, acquire new information, and make new contacts through their participation. Employees who join corrective action teams will have new opportunities to learn problem solving as well as observe the skills of others. From working as a team, the members will also be sharing information, not only of a technical nature, but about the organization and themselves. The contacts made on corrective action teams will help people learn about new sources of information, resources, and support elsewhere in the organization.

Problem-solving teams are an integral part of the Corrective Action Process. They may be established on any level of the organization, but are always created by a manager or supervisor. A team is assembled to work on a specific problem and eliminate it. The membership may vary, depending on the type of problem you are attempting to resolve, but the team may include persons from one or more areas and departments.

When a problem-solving team is formed, a chairperson should be appointed who is responsible for running the meetings and making sure that the work gets done. The problem-solving team will continue to meet on a regular basis until the problem is resolved.

The members of the team must have a clear understanding of what is expected of them and of the time frame involved. Members of the team should also possess the necessary skills to fulfill their charter. This means having the right kind of people skills to function effectively as a team as well as the necessary technical skills to solve the problem. Management support is critical for a team to work. It is the job of the manager to provide as much support as possible to assist the team, providing it with any necessary resources and information, perhaps balancing the team members' other work responsibilities when there is a danger of overload. Finally, training may be required for employees to be able to contribute effectively to a team operation. This may include training in group problem solving, statistics for measurement, and the "how to's" of implementation.

You will need to decide whether a problem-solving team should be composed of persons from within your area/department only or have cross-organizational membership. If the causes of the problem are local, your people have the necessary expertise, information, and resources to resolve it, and the political consequences are minimal, then a team should be formed in your organization. When this isn't the case, the team should always include persons from outside your organization. The following are some guidelines that can help you to make this decision.

Use intraorganizational teams when:
- Causes of the problem are confined to your organization.
- Necessary expertise and information is located in your organization.
- Resources required to solve the problem (staff, time, equipment, materials, etc.) are minimal or may be found in your organization.
- Problem interdependency (number of others who would be affected directly by changes) is low.
- Political consequences are minimal (few people outside your organization have a direct stake in the outcome, or will offer resistance or try to influence problem resolution).

Use interorganizational teams when:
- Some of the causes of the problem may be found in another organization.
- Persons in another organization have the necessary expertise or information to solve the problem.
- Problem interdependency is high.

- Political consequences are great — others need to be involved who are potential stakeholders.
- Resources required to solve the problem are fairly extensive — it may be necessary to pool resources among several organizations.

As a manager you still have some important responsibilities when a problem-solving team is formed, and much of the group's success will depend on how well you follow these guidelines. Make sure that everyone on the problem solving team understands the ground rules. Define your expectations up front. Don't overload members of the team so that they can't do a good job on their regular tasks or contribute effectively to the team. Empower the team whenever possible by providing them with any necessary resources, information, and support from either yourself or other managers, and give the problem-solving team as much autonomy as you can.

Keep in mind these important factors when assigning responsibility for problem solving:

- Does someone already have this area as an assignment?
- How great is the time pressure?
- Would this issue benefit from new perspectives?
- How much controversy surrounds the issue?
- Does this problem involve a great deal of interdependency with other organizational units?
- Would participation in solving the problem help in the development of others?
- Do the people in your work area possess enough resources and information to adequately resolve the problem?

<u>Solve a problem yourself when:</u>

- There is a clear solution.

- You have an explicit mandate to solve these types of problems.

- You possess more expertise to solve the problem, i.e., the problem calls for someone with specialized knowledge and you have the appropriate background, education, or experience.

- No one else is overly concerned about the problem or would have their own skills enhanced and developed by assisting you. The problem may be uninteresting to others and they wouldn't learn much from working on it.

- The issue is relatively routine, i.e., something you deal with on a regular basis.

- Time constraints are great — quick action is required and you would not have enough time to delegate or put a team together.

- You need to exercise control not only over the results, but ways in which these results are obtained. You may need to direct the implementation of the solution — who is involved, the tasks carried out, the sequence of steps, etc.

<u>If you do this, remember to:</u>

- Act quickly.

- Notify others.

- Involve others to some extent, but don't "volunteer" them.

When to Solve a Problem Yourself

Delegate a problem to an individual or existing group when:

- The person or group has clear expertise to solve the problem.

- The person or group already has this area as part of their assigned responsibility.

- The problem can be solved at a lower level.

- Persons under you possess the necessary information and resources to solve the problem.

- Some individual or group shows real interest in tackling this problem.

- A team has previously worked on this or a related problem.

- Your boss or other managers do not expect you personally to solve the problem.

- Time pressures are moderate, but manageable (the more time available, the better).

- The outcome and results are clearly specified or known, but the means to achieve these can be decided by someone other than yourself.

- There is low interdependency — few or no other departments or organizations are involved.

If you do this, remember to:

- Communicate expectations clearly.

- Review progress regularly.

- Keep others informed.

- Reward participants.

- Act quickly on recommendations.

When to Delegate a Problem

Form a new problem-solving team when:

- Others can gain expertise or demonstrate their knowledge in solving the problem — if they have experience and ideas, they should be used as resources.
- A consensus can be built around an issue and those who are affected by the problem can participate in its resolution.
- A variety of interests are represented, especially if there are conflicting points of view.
- An opportunity and adequate time to study a problem and come up with the best possible solution are provided.
- People are allowed to develop their skills, acquire new information, and make new contacts through their particpation.

Use intraorganizational teams when:

- Causes of the problem are confined to your organization.
- Necessary expertise and information is located in your organization.
- Resources required to solve the problem (staff, time, equipment, materials, etc.) are minimal or may be found in your organization.
- Problem interdependency (number of others who would be affected directly by changes) is low.
- Political consequences are minimal (few people outside your organization have a direct stake in the outcome, may offer resistance, try to influence problem resolution).

Use interorganizational teams when:

- Some of the causes of the problem may be found in another organization.
- Persons in another organization have the necessary expertise or information to solve the problem.
- Problem interdependency is high.
- Political consequences are great — others who are potential stakeholders need to be involved.
- Resources required to solve the problem are fairly extensive — it may be necessary to pool resources among several organizations.

When to Form a New Problem-Solving Team

Step 4 — Application of
Problem-Solving Techniques

Corrective action requires an almost continual process of intensive problem solving on the part of everybody involved and at every step of the way from the start of problem identification to the last stage of implementation. Thus, while we have named the fourth step of the Corrective Action Process as the problem-solving step, the analytic techniques described here can and should be applied every step of the way. However, the fourth step will entail more problem solving than the rest, since the exploration of alternative causes of the problem and alternative solutions is the focus of this stage.

This section describes a variety of analytic techniques that individuals and problem-solving teams may choose to use as they wish, rather than specifying a rigid set of steps to be applied in every case. Later sections of this book describe group process techniques such as brainstorming and ways to make meetings effective. Refer to them for the *process* side and use this section for analysis tools. Thus, it will be up to the reader to determine which of the techniques would be most appropriate given the nature of the problem being examined and the experience and inclinations of those engaged in the problem-solving activity.

While we all engage in a variety of forms of problem solving as a daily part of our work, some readers may not be familiar with some of the more rigorous analytic techniques that can significantly improve our ability to solve problems. Some readers may be well versed in other analytic techniques that could be used in Step 4 and we encourage them to use such techniques as appropriate. The techniques described here are not meant to be the definitive list, but rather to offer some of the more common and useful methods. The point is to solve the quality and productivity problems at hand, and the method used is of less concern as long as it serves the purpose.

One word of caution: It is wise to devote a considerable amount of time to the task of determining the causes of a problem before leaping into the more appealing task of solving the problem. It is human nature to move quickly to try to resolve a problem; however, an in-depth exploration of alternative causes of the problem will generally lead to a far more targeted and effective solution. Therefore, a problem-solving team or an individual assigned to solve a problem should plan on spending at least a few meetings exclusively on the exploration of possible causes before moving onto the resolution of the problem.

Thus, the problem-solving step may be seen as being composed of four parts:

1. Exploration of alternative causes
2. Determination of the primary causes
3. Exploration of alternative solutions
4. Choosing the best solution (or a few options)

In this section we will describe methods for visualizing and displaying data as well as methods for analyzing the data. Some methods for visualizing and displaying data are:

- Checklists
- Time Charts
- Line Charts
- Bar Graphs
- Pie Charts

The methods for analyzing data that we present are:

- Pareto Analysis (presented in Step 2)
- Process Analysis
- Cause and Effect Diagram
- Force Field Analysis

Methods of Visualizing and Displaying Data

Checklists may be used as a way to gather data which can then be displayed through graphic means or used by itself as a tool to discover significant trends and patterns. Checklists can be used to note and track the occurrence of any event and to compare the patterns of occurrence associated with different variables. It is often possible to discover the source of a problem simply by composing and then examining a checklist.

The key to success in using checklists (in addition to accuracy) is to think carefully about the type of event that should be tracked and the most relevant variables. Checklists can note the following:

- Frequency of occurrence during a given time period
- Cost
- Revenue
- Length of time to accomplish
- Success/failure
- Number and type of people involved
- Aspect of product/service

Figure 2.4 shows checklists that can be used to compare the performance of sales representatives in different regions.

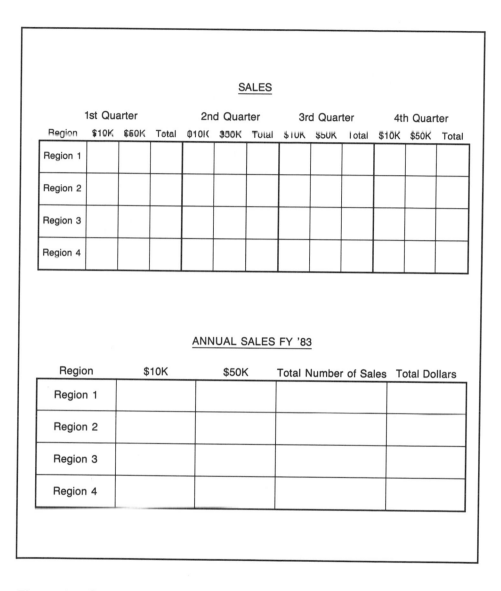

SALES

	1st Quarter			2nd Quarter			3rd Quarter			4th Quarter		
Region	$10K	$50K	Total	$10K	$50K	Total	$10K	$50K	Total	$10K	$50K	Total
Region 1												
Region 2												
Region 3												
Region 4												

ANNUAL SALES FY '83

Region	$10K	$50K	Total Number of Sales	Total Dollars
Region 1				
Region 2				
Region 3				
Region 4				

Figure 2.4 Checklists Used to Compare Sales Performance

These checklists could be used to compare the performance of different regions, differences in sales per quarter, differences in the number of sales per size of sale, and so on. A pattern which revealed that Region 3 outstripping the others in performance would provide a clue for a direction to pursue to gather more information to help solve the overall sales problem.

Time charts, line charts, pie charts, and bar graphs can be used to display the data you collect graphically. Graphic illustrations are useful in helping you to discover trends and patterns as well as to present your findings and conclusions to others, such as the management to which you or your team is accountable.

Time charts display the time period during which the events with which you are concerned occurred. Time charts can be used to illustrate the periods during which different activities took place (or will take place), as well as to show different types or levels of activities which have occurred at different points in time. Figure 2.5 shows an example of the way time charts can be used.

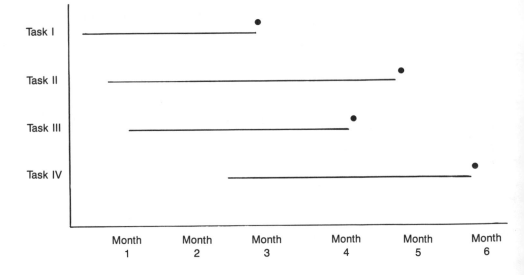

Figure 2.5 Time Chart

Line charts are versatile and useful means for describing and comparing information that can be quantified. They can be used to illustrate trends over time, the relationship between the occurrence of an event and a variable, and the comparison of trends and relationships. Figures 2.6 and 2.7 are examples of line charts.

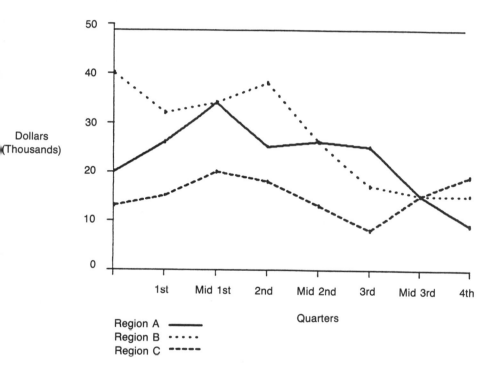

Figure 2.6 Line Chart Showing Sales by Quarter and Region

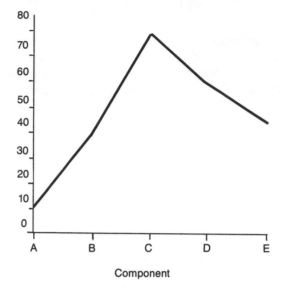

Figure 2.7 Line Chart Showing Average Number of Defects by Component

Pie charts are most appropriate to use when you wish to examine or display the relationship of all the elements of something to each other and to the whole. The parts are displayed as a percentage of the whole. This technique is useful when examining an event or activities with no more than eight elements, as more than that is visually difficult to comprehend. Figure 2.8 is an example of a pie chart.

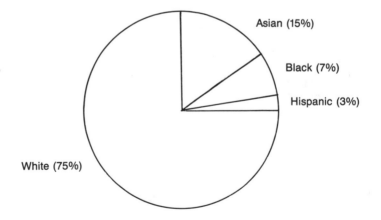

Figure 2.8 Pie Chart Showing Racial Composition of Level II Managers

Bar graphs are useful in showing comparisons between and among events or items. It is the easiest type of graphic illustration to compose and to understand. A variety of techniques may be used to convey emphasis on different aspects of the information displayed. Figures 2.9 and 2.10 are examples of bar charts.

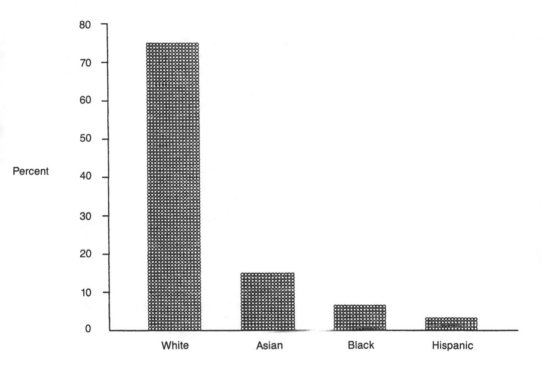

Figure 2.9 Bar Graph Showing Racial Composition of Level II Managers

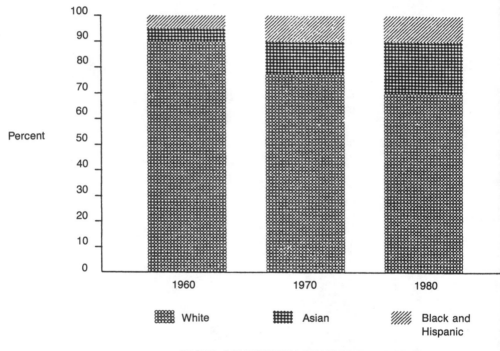

RACIAL COMPOSITION OF LEVEL II MANAGERS

Figure 2.10 Racial Composition of Level II Managers

Analytic Techniques*

Process analysis is a technique to help in understanding all the steps and relationships involved in producing a product or providing a service. It can also help in analyzing the sources of problems and potential for improvement in the ways that your organization currently operates. The objective of process analysis is to discover whether the process that you now use is capable in its current form of turning out a quality product/service or of improved productivity. If you learn that it is not, then you can use process analysis to identify where changes need to be made. Of course, once you have implemented the changes you should monitor the results to see if the improvements expected have occurred. If they have not, you may wish to repeat the process analysis to see if other causes of the problem or steps in the process were missed.

Process analysis can be considered as an extension of industrial engineering concepts in a nonmanufacturing environment. For the best results, it should be conducted in a participative, nonthreatening fashion, so that everyone feels free to fully examine whatever problems may exist.

The flow diagram is the primary method you can use to conduct the process analysis. The first step is to outline the relationship of your organization to the vendor and to the customer in providing a service or producing a product.

The next step is to identify the activities and functions that you or those in your work area perform to provide the service or product. In other words, the point is to focus in on your part of the process. There may be other complex interdependencies with other parts of your organization or several vendors and all of these should be carefully outlined.

Once you have identified your part in the process, you and your team should construct a flow diagram with as much detail as possible which graphically illustrates all the operations, actions, steps, and decision points that are involved in the process from start to finish. Be as comprehensive as possible.

The last step in process analysis is to review the completed flow chart and to identify the points where problems exist that currently hinder your organization's ability to improve productivity or produce quality products and services.

---

*Pareto analysis is covered in *Step 2 — Problem Classification*.

A flow chart can use a variety of symbols to indicate different activities, decision points, results, and movement (Figure 2.11). Figure 2.12 shows a flow diagram for use in process analysis.

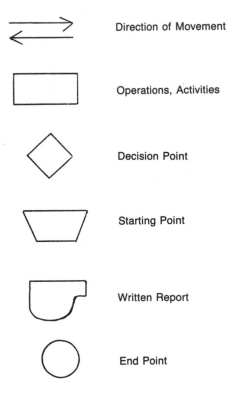

Direction of Movement

Operations, Activities

Decision Point

Starting Point

Written Report

End Point

Figure 2.11 Common Symbols Used in Flow Charts

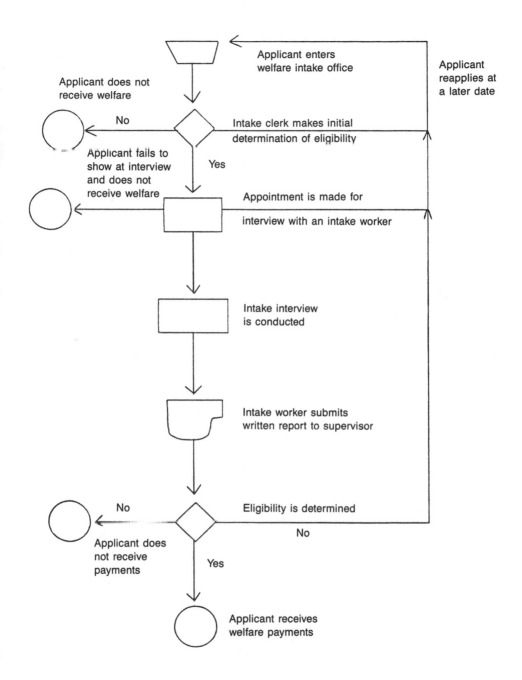

Figure 2.12 Process Analysis Flow Chart

The *cause and effect diagram* (also known as an Ishikawa or fishbone diagram) is a well-known technique useful in illustrating the relationship between the range of potential causes of a problem and the problem itself. It is used as a way to organize the responses that you receive when brainstorming about the potential causes of a problem.

The cause and effect diagram is composed of lines designed to represent the relationship between an outcome, event, result, or effect and the potential causes of the effect. The potential causes are the "ribs" of the "fish." The causes are classified into categories and labeled on the ribs. There may be further subcategories of causes that may be represented as branches on the ribs. The cause and effect diagram does not actually help you to solve a problem, but is does provide a systematic way to array the variety of potential causes and to view their relationships with the problem and each other. Once having displayed these causes, it is up to the team or individual to assess their relative importance and to decide which ones deserve further examination.

The cause and effect diagram is a fairly straightforward process involving three steps. In the first step the problem, event, or result is entered into a box which is placed at the far right of the paper or blackboard. A horizontal line is drawn across the page and ends at the problem box. Ribs are then drawn above and below the line and are used to represent the major categories of causes of the problems. These categories should be developed through brainstorming. Major categories generally cover topics such as human resources, finances, equipment, and procedures. Figure 2.13 shows a cause and effect diagram at this stage of the process.

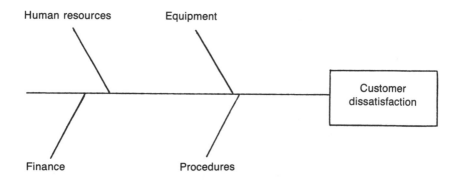

Figure 2.13 First Stage of a Cause and Effect Diagram

In the second step the subcategories of causes are identified through brainstorming and then arrayed on the appropriate ribs of the diagram. The best approach to take is to brainstorm around each major cause individually, rather than all at once. During stage two you may discover new major categories of causes which can be added as extra ribs. If possible, you should try to indicate the relationships that exist among causes when you discover these. Figure 2.14 shows a cause and effect diagram at this stage of the process.

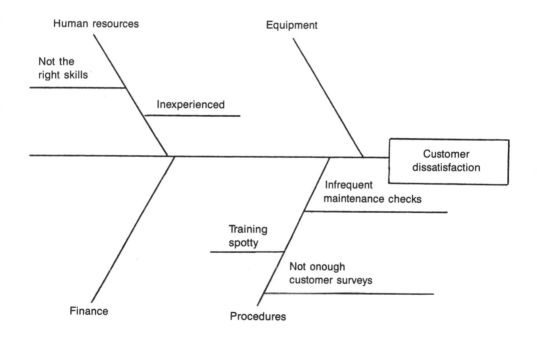

Figure 2.14 Second Stage of a Cause and Effect Diagram

In the final step the team or individual should consider the relative importance of the various causes of the problem. A variety of things may occur at this stage. Some causes may be dismissed because the team or individual has no control over them, while others are widely acknowledged to have a relatively minor impact on the problem. Alternatively, there may be a set of potential causes about which more needs to be known; for example, while their impact is believed to be great, no data have been gathered to substantiate that perception. In this case, the diagram can be used to identify those areas in which further research should be conducted. A team may also discover at this point that many of the potential causes are partially controlled or influenced by other groups and people, and that they will need to gain the cooperation of these people to address the problem or even to fully understand the impact of the causes. Figure 2.15 shows a cause and effect diagram at the final stage of the process.

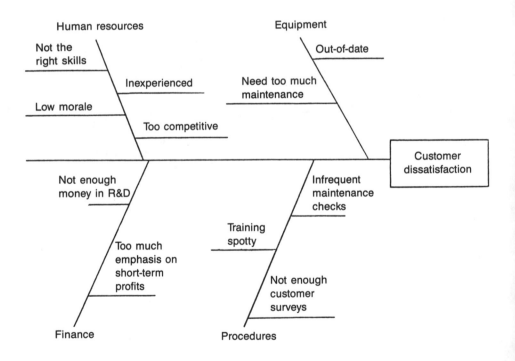

Figure 2.15 Final Stage of a Cause and Effect Diagram

Force field analysis looks at the issue of how to analyze and solve problems differently. In contrast to the cause and effect diagram, force field analysis examines both the causes of a problem and those factors which mitigate the problem or could potentially improve the situation. Thus, with this method one examines those forces that hinder the organization from reaching a particular quality or productivity goal and those that can or do help it to reach that goal.

Force field analysis is concerned with four elements: the situation or problem as it stands, the goal or desired state, helping forces, and hindering forces. Force field analysis provides a systematic way to identify these elements and to strategize about how to manipulate or influence them to improve the current situation and to solve the problem at hand.

There are three primary ways to change the situation from its current status to the desired one. First, you can decrease the number or impact of the hindering forces. Second, conversely, you can increase the number or impact of the helping forces. And third, you can do both at the same time. In general, the last option is the one that most people and groups follow. The primary challenge with this method is determining the relative strength, weakness, and impact of the helping and hindering forces in order to determine which ones to change.

A useful thing to note is that force field analysis is probably the best method to use when dealing with subjective data which are difficult or impossible to quantify, such as morale, climate, and management effectiveness.

Figure 2.16 shows the format you should use in conducting a force field analysis.

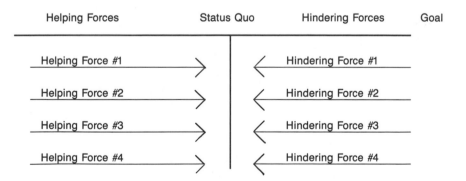

Figure 2.16 Force Field Analysis Form

There are four major steps in conducting a force field analysis. The first step is to define both the current problem and the desired change, result, or new status. Enter these in the appropriate places on the form. The second step is to identify the factors in the environment that are hindering forces (contributing to the problem, preventing its resolution, etc.) and those that are helping forces (mitigating the negative effects of the problem, moving the situation toward the desired state, etc.). A brainstorming session to elicit all of the possible helping and hindering forces would be helpful. A secondary step would be to examine and identify the relationships among and between the helping and hindering forces. The third step is to assess the relative strength and weakness of each of the forces. This can be done by assigning them a number on a scale you have devised. The last step is to decide which of the helping and hindering forces should be changed in order to have the greatest chance of achieving the desired changes in quality or productivity. Some things you or your team might consider are:

- Which forces have the greatest impact?
- Which do you have control over?
- Which would be easy to influence?
- Which require further analysis to understand?
- How long will it take to change?
- How much will it cost?

Step 5 — Implementation

The final step in the Corrective Action Process is implementation. This step is critical because it is at this point that your ideas, analysis, and solutions get translated into action. Implementation means creating action steps that specify how your solution will be put to work. This section will discuss the use of the Corrective Action Report, the specific skills needed for implementation, and how to handle resistance to change, since in many cases the ideas you and your team come up with will require changes in the way that people do their work.

Implementation really begins with the final result of the problem-solving process, which is the Corrective Action Report. In this report the problem solver (who may or may not be the manager) or the problem-solving team will discuss your solution to the problem in depth, and provide information about the following:

- What should be changed (e.g., technical requirements, scheduling, staffing, etc.)?
- How long will it take to implement the solution?
- What steps will be taken to implement the solution?
- What will be the expense of implementing the solution?
- Who is responsible for implementing the solution?
- What measurement criteria can be established?
- What effect will the solution have on product or service costs, or cost of quality?

Corrective action will not work and you will not achieve your goals unless there is a timely and effective implementation of your solution. Needless to say, good solutions have absolutely no value and are worth nothing to your organization if they cannot be put into use. Unfortunately, a surprising number of good ideas go nowhere and gather dust on a manager's shelf, simply because the implementation step was either neglected or poorly thought through. Everyone knows of examples of good solutions or terrific reports never used. Thus, implementation is a key part of your job in the quality process — the work is not through until you have managed a solution all the way through its implementation stage. In many ways, as all innovators know, this can be the hardest part!

In order to manage the implementation stage, you need to have skills in dealing with three important areas:

1. People — your staff and other persons who possess important information and resources, but who are not under your jurisdiction; you must have ways to involve them and engage their interest and skills while balancing the demands on their time.
2. Projects — the technical and administrative side; putting the right pieces of the solution together in the right order, keeping things moving, meeting deadlines, etc.
3. "Politics" — managing the important interests and stakeholders who may influence the outcome of your solution. This requires being sensitive to others who have a vital interest and stake in what you're doing, "selling" them on the importance of your project, and getting their backing where it helps you to achieve your goal.

In most cases, corrective action will not be "isolated action" with one or two people off in a corner trying to fix some problem. Usually, it will require the cooperative effort of many people, each handling some part of the process, but mutually interdependent with others in order to achieve success. The key players in the corrective action process are:

- The *problem identifiers*, who may first notice that something is wrong.
- The *managers* responsible for seeing that something is done.
- The *problem solvers*, whether this is a specific manager, an individual to whom the problem has been delegated, or a problem-solving team.
- The *implementers*, who are ultimately responsible for taking corrective action.

(See Figure 2.17.)

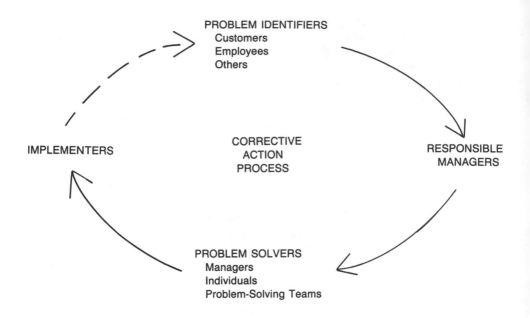

Figure 2.17 Key Players in Implementation

The cycle is complete when the solution is implemented and the problem has disappeared.

The following items are important to effective implementation and include some steps you may need to take:

- Action for recommendations should be timely. People have many expectations after putting in time on problem solving and you will be able to use the momentum from their efforts if you act quickly.
- Implementers should be identified. Don't assume that someone will just "do it"; pinpoint the responsibility for taking the action steps.
- Implementers must be informed. Get the message across clearly to those responsible for the implememtation and make sure they understand their role.
- Necessary approvals need to be secured. Don't rush off and take action before approval has been obtained from other managers or parties who may be affected or need to give some type of "blessing," even if it's just a formality.
- Necessary resources must be secured. In many cases corrective action will require using additional resources, such as staff, time, equipment, funds, etc. Try to secure resources up front so that corrective action won't be stalled later on.

- Make sure affected parties are participating. This is one of the skills of managing "politics" and requires not only being aware of *who* the affected parties are, but finding ways to involve them and allow them to participate so they won't become adversaries at a later stage.
- New requirements for providing services or producing products should be clearly understood. If you are defining requirements, or adding some new ones, make certain people understand these up front and what this means for their work.
- It may be necessary to have new or additional training for your staff, so be sure that it is appropriate to the tasks they are expected to perform. Implementation often fails even though employees are committed and eager to begin, but because they lack the necessary skills to carry out the corrective action. In many cases, this is easily overcome by setting up the necessary training.
- New actions should be clearly tied to measurements so that you have some way of judging the impact of corrective action and knowing that your efforts are working to improve performance.
- Actions likewise should be followed up and monitored so that you will know they are on track. If people begin to stray, you can set them on the right course again.
- Establish checkpoints along the way to facilitate the monitoring process and help people learn to evaluate themselves. These checkpoints should be reasonable performance goals that will tell you and others involved in corrective action if they are really solving the problem and doing it on time.
- In almost all cases, you should expect to make mid-course adjustments, i.e., fine-tuning of your corrective action strategy. Since work conditions and organizations never remain the same, it is reasonable to modify your problem solving and implementation strategy in small ways to correct for this.
- The problem identifiers should always get feedback in one form or another about the changes that are taking place. This way, they will know that their efforts to identify problems have made an impact and were taken seriously, and it will encourage them to watch out for other problems in the future.
- Finally, be sure to recognize the problem solvers and implementers; give them credit and rewards when it is appropriate to let them know their work was appreciated. This will also help to motivate others when they see that problem solvers are getting greater visibility in their area or department.

Two key aspects of implementation that are often overlooked but are important to your success are timely action on recommendations and giving feedback to problem identifiers. Both of these will provide you with credibility and show that you are serious about the quality process. It will also make people feel responded to and thus raise morale. Be sure not to leave them out of your implementation steps.

To facilitate this step you can use the Implementation Checklist (Figure 2.18). The first part concerns major items you will need to consider before implementation gets underway. This includes the specific implementers, getting approvals from the necessary managers, securing the appropriate resources, and determining who the affected parties will be. The second part of the Implementation Checklist (Figure 2.19) is a more detailed PERT chart, and includes the specific steps you need to consider for effective implementation. For each of these steps you should determine the date it will be initiated, who will be responsible for this activity, and the date to be completed. This should be done for the entire period of implementation from the initial briefing of implementers through the final recognition for participants.

Another tool for implementing corrective action is the Problem Tracking Form (Figure 2.20) that may be used in conjunction with the Implementation Checklist. By using all three of these forms you will be able to implement and track solutions to problems in your work area. The Problem Tracking Form provides you with a useful summary of your total effort on a particular problem, including:

- How it impacts your organization.
- The probable causes of the problem.
- Who is assigned responsibility for developing corrective action.
- What action is to be taken.
- Who is responsible for implementing the action steps.
- The estimated completion date.
- The problem's status along the way.

In almost all cases, implementation will involve some type of change — how people do their work, who they work with, etc. Since work habits are usually difficult to alter, you should expect to encounter some resistance. We all have faced this at one time or another. Implementation involves change and resistance to change is well known. Thus, it is important to learn how to deal effectively with resistance.

	People or Items Needed	Date Obtained
Implementers		
Approvals		
Resources		
Affected Parties		

Figure 2.18 Implementation Checklist — People or Items Needed
(Copyright © 1983 Goodmeasure, Inc. Cambridge, MA. All rights reserved.)

	Date to Be Initiated	Responsible Person	Date to Be Completed
Briefing of Implementers			
Notification of Affected Parties			
Communication of New Requirements			
Training			
Measurements			
Checkpoints			
Mid-Course Adjustments			
Feedback to Problem Identifiers			
Recognition			

Figure 2.19 Implementation Checklist — Activities
(Copyright © 1983 Goodmeasure, Inc. Cambridge, MA. All rights reserved.)

The Problem	Impact on Your Organization	Probable Causes (Problems)	Assigned Responsibility for Development of Corrective Action	Required Corrective Action	Assigned Responsibility for Resolution	Estimated Resolution Date	Status

Figure 2.20 Problem Tracking Form

There are a number of things you can do to minimize and overcome resistance to change and build commitment to change. Many of these things can be done *ahead of time*:

- Allow room for participation in the planning of the change. It is much less traumatic for people when change is something they *do* rather than something *done* to them.
- Leave some choices within the overall decision to change. Decide ahead of time some of the discretionary areas of change where people may still have choices and where there may be some alternatives that will still accomplish your change goal.
- Provide a clear picture of the change — a "vision" with details about the new state. This gives people an idea of the shape of the new organization, helps them to see past the short run, and provides an image that can help "pull" people along.
- Share information about changes to the fullest extent possible. The more secrecy there is, the less cooperation you're likely to get, and the anxiety level will undoubtedly rise.

During the change process there are several things you can do:

- Divide a big change into more manageable and familiar steps. Let people take small steps first. This will make the change seem less overwhelming and more within the grasp of your employees. Once the first step is taken, the others will follow more easily.
- Minimize surprises. Give people warning about new requirements. If you can share information along the way as you hear about it, there will be fewer big shocks for people to absorb. In many cases, the change will proceed much more smoothly when surprises are avoided.
- Allow change requests to digest. Give people a chance to become accustomed to the idea of change before making a commitment. Don't expect instant enthusiasm and acceptance of the change by all parties; allow some time for the idea to sink in so that people can make their own commitment.
- Demonstrate your own commitment to the change repeatedly. Your own behavior toward the change will have a significant impact on how much others believe in and implement the change. Be a positive model.
- Make standards and requirements clear of exactly what is expected of people. Be concise and specific about what performance and behavior you expect from employees. This will help them grasp the change better and provide you with some benchmarks to measure how well the change has taken hold.
- Offer positive reinforcement for competence; let people know they "can do it." You may have to give some extra encouragement during the first part of a change effort; this will help people get past the initial uncertainty.

- Look for and reward pioneers, innovators, and early successes to serve as models. This will show the rest of your employees that change can take place and that it is not an impossible task. Some "pioneers" may even have made a headstart on the others before anyone realized an official change was taking place.
- Help people find the extra time and energy they may need to get through the change. This may require shifting assignments or tasks. Also try to build some synergy among your people, and get them to function as a team and build group commitment to the change.
- Avoid creating obvious "losers" from the change. Change does not have to be a "zero sum" game with both losers and winners. Some people may benefit much more than others, but help your people to see change as an opportunity — not just a loss.
- Allow a legitimate expression of nostalgia and grief for the past, then create excitement about the future. People need time to work through their grief and sadness about the past, but they need to feel excited about the opportunities, challenge, and new possibilities of the future.

All of these things will help make people more comfortable with the change and less likely to work against it. That in turn will support your hard work to improve quality in the products and services of your areas or departments.

Recommendations for problem solving should include answers to these questions:

- What should be changed (e.g., technical requirements, scheduling, staffing, etc.)?

- How long will it take to implement the solution?

- What steps will be taken to implement the solution?

- What will be the expense of implementing the solution?

- Who is responsible for implementing the solution?

- What measurement criteria can be established?

- What effect will the solution have on the cost of the product or service, or the cost of quality?

Guidelines for Corrective Action Reporting
(Copyright © Goodmeasure, Inc. Cambridge, MA. All rights reserved.)

Take timely action on recommendations.

Inform implementers. Don't assume that someone will just "do it"; pinpoint the responsibility for taking the action steps.

Implementers must be informed; make sure they understand their role.

Secure necessary approvals from other managers or parties who may be affected.

Secure necessary resources: staff, time, equipment, funds, etc. (Try to get resources up front so that action won't be stalled later on.)

Make sure affected parties are participating so they won't become adversaries at a later stage.

Communicate clearly new standards or requirements for providing services or producing products so that they are well understood. Make certain your people understand these up front and what this means for their work.

Develop any new or additional training for your people.

Tie new actions clearly to measurements so that you have some way of judging the impact of corrective action and know that your efforts are working to improve performance.

Follow up and monitor actions so that you will know they are on track, or if people begin to stray, you can set them on the right course again.

Establish checkpoints along the way — reasonable performance goals that will tell you and others involved in corrective action if they are really solving the problem and doing it on time.

Make mid-course adjustments — some fine-tuning of your strategy for corrective action.

Get feedback to the problem identifiers about the changes that are taking place. This way, they will know that their efforts to identify problems have made an impact and were taken seriously, and it will encourage them to watch out for other problems in the future.

Recognize the problem solvers and implementers; give them credit and rewards where it is appropriate to let them know their work was appreciated.

Guidelines for Effective Implementation

Allow room for participation in the planning of the change.

Leave choices within the overall decision to change.

Provide a clear picture of the change; reduce uncertainty and fantasy.

Share information.

Divide a big change into manageable smaller steps.

Minimize surprises and provide advance warning.

Demonstrate your own commitment to the change repeatedly.

Make standards and requirements clear.

Encourage and reward people's competence; let them know they *can* do it.

Identify and reward early successes.

Help people find the extra time and energy they need for change.

Avoid creating obvious "losers" from the change.

Allow legitimate expression of nostalgia and grief for the past, then encourage excitement about the opportunities of the future.

Building Commitment to Change

PART THREE
GETTING ORGANIZED FOR ACTION

The Basic Framework for Problem-Solving Teams

Roles and Responsibilities for Teams and Other People Involved in Quality/Productivity Improvement

Problem-Solving Teams

Problem-solving teams are one of the primary vehicles for providing solutions to quality and productivity problems. A problem-solving team may be formed by any level of management to resolve any type of problem that cannot be corrected by an individual supervisor.

In general, a major objective of the Corrective Action Process should be to resolve problems at the lowest possible organizational level. Whenever possible, problem-solving teams should be formed to deal with problems within one division or operation. The larger the problem scope in terms of the numbers of organizations adversely affected or required for solution implementation, the higher the organizational level at which the problem-solving team will have to be formed. In those instances where problems are of such scope that they affect more than one division, function, or operation of your organization, a final recommendation to form an interdivisional problem-solving team should be made in writing to the appropriate person (i.e., a vice-president or general manager). The problem-solving team is responsible for undertaking every aspect of the process of researching, analyzing, and solving the problem it has been assigned. Thus, the team will be involved and in control from the start — clarifying the problem, to the finish — recommending a permanent solution. The major elements of a problem-solving team's responsibilities are as follows:

1. Complete a clear statement of the problem to be investigated — its scope and background, and its effect on the organization or organizations involved.
2. Estimate the current annual cost incurred because of the problem. Non-quantitative statements of the subjective effects of the problem may also be included.
3. Investigate potential causes of and solutions to the problem across all organizational lines and levels if necessary.
4. Select from those solutions the one that is most capable of implementation, is cost-effective, and provides a permanent solution to the stated problem.
5. Estimate the cost of the solution implementation as accurately as possible.
6. Incorporate the previously mentioned information into a written report with

recommendations to the management level responsible for the formation of the problem-solving team.

7. Once the final written report and recommendation is submitted to the management level responsible for formation of the problem-solving team, the team should be prepared to present its findings and recommendations to the appropriate level staff meeting if so requested. Once this action is complete the problem-solving team may be disbanded, unless further direction is received from management.

Team Members

For the most part, the responsibility of problem-solving team members coincides with the overall responsibilities of the team. The most important point to keep in mind is that each member should feel fully responsible for the success and progress of the entire team. This principle supports what should be one of the major objectives of any quality or productivity improvement program — greater participation by everyone in identifying and solving problems. Problem-solving teams provide an effective vehicle for promoting participation. However, little will be accomplished if each team member fails to fulfill his or her responsibility to participate fully.

Later sections will describe the roles and responsibilities of teams in greater detail. The following is a summary of the overall responsibilities of team members:

- Be fully responsible for the success, progress, and output of the team.
- Participate fully in the team.
- Fulfill assigned team responsibilities.
- Attend every meeting, if possible.
- Be an effective participant.
- Raise important issues actively rather than passively following the direction set by the chair or other members.

Chairs or Team Leaders

The role and responsibility of a problem-solving team chair or leader may vary considerably depending on how much the team will participate. This will depend in large part on the skills and inclinations of the person designated the chair as well as the ease with which a team works together. In some cases, the chair may take a firm leadership role, whereas in others he or she may take a role more similar to that of facilitator or discussion leader.

Regardless of the extent to which the chair and team choose to participate, the chair will have ultimate responsibility for the following:

- Set the schedule for meetings.
- Call meetings.
- Keep meetings on time.

- Keep team progress on track.
- Keep discussions on the topic.
- Encourage full participation.
- Foster a positive team spirit.
- Represent the team and communicate with the relevant levels of management.
- Represent the team and communicate with other people and groups.
- Ensure that the team makes clear decisions and votes on them.
- Lead the presentation to management.
- Take ultimate responsibility for team decisions, progress, and outcomes.

Later sections explain in greater depth what is entailed in fulfilling these responsibilities.

Managers

The managers who supervise problem-solving teams also have a set of responsibilities to fulfill. Managers may have full or shared responsibility for supervising a team depending on whether the team is composed entirely of their subordinates or whether the team crosses organizational or work areas. In the latter case, the manager may be sharing responsibility with one or more managers or may be part of a Corrective Action Steering Committee.

In any case, managers have responsibility for the following:

- Charter problem-solving teams.
- Agree to release subordinates to join teams that cross organizational lines.
- Set clear constraints and boundaries as appropriate regarding the problem to be addressed, research methodology, the range of options for solutions, etc.
- Allocate the necessary resources (time, people, budget) to support the team.
- Actively support the team in their own work area and elsewhere as needed.
- Inform the team about relevant issues and changes in circumstances and the environment.
- Stay involved in and informed about team activities, plans, and progress.
- Inform others (at all levels) about team activities, plans, and progress.
- Decide whether or not to accept the team's recommendations.
- Decide when and how to implement accepted recommendations.
- Provide rewards and recognition for teams and team members.

Corrective Action Steering Committee

A Corrective Action Steering Committee should be established if an improvement program is occurring on an organization-wide basis to oversee and direct the process. Its membership should include the general manager or appropriate executive, his or her direct reports, and any other designated representatives. A steering committee is chartered to create organization-wide policy, to oversee and guide the activities of the teams, and to assure that all of these are consistent with overall policies and plans with regard to quality or productivity improvement in the organization. The steering committee will also provide high level management commitment for the process and make sure all necessary resources are available to implement quality/productivity improvement activities.

The specific responsibilities of the Corrective Action Steering Committee include the following:

- Establish and approve division-wide quality/productivity policy.
- Provide high-level visibility, leadership, and direction to the Quality/Productivity Improvement Program.
- Review progress of implementation and continuation plans at regularly scheduled meetings.
- Ensure that quality/productivity planning is consistent with the human resource thrust for organizational effectiveness.
- Review and approve annual, long range, and strategic plan quality/productivity goals and objectives.
- Demonstrate continued commitment to quality/productivity improvement — in both action and communications.

Create a statement of the problem.

Estimate the costs of the problem.

Investigate potential causes and solutions.

Select the solution that is most cost-effective, and is capable of implementation and provides a permanent solution.

Estimate the cost of implementing the solution.

Present recommendations to management.

Problem-Solving Team Responsibilities

Be fully responsible for success, progress, and output of the team.

Participate in the team fully.

Fulfill assigned team responsibilities.

Attend every meeting, if possible.

Be an effective participant.

Raise important issues actively rather than passively following the direction set by the chair or other members.

Team Member Responsibilities

Set the schedule for meetings.

Call meetings.

Keep meetings on time.

Keep team progress on track.

Keep discussion on the topic.

Encourage full participation.

Foster a positive team spirit.

Represent the team and communicate with the relevant levels of management.

Ensure that the team makes clear decisions and votes on them.

Lead the presentation to management.

Take ultimate responsibility for team decisions, progress, and outcomes.

Chair or Team Leader Responsibilities

Charter problem-solving teams.

Agree to release subordinates to join teams that cross organizational lines.

Set clear constraints and boundaries as appropriate regarding the problem to be addressed, research methodology, the range of options for solutions, etc.

Allocate the necessary resources (time, people, and budget) to support the team.

Actively support the team in your own work area and elsewhere as needed.

Inform the team about relevant issues and changes in circumstances and the environment.

Stay involved in and informed about team activities, plans, and progress.

Inform others (at all levels) about team activities, plans, and progress.

Decide whether or not to accept the team's recommendations.

Decide when and how to implement the recommendations that have been accepted.

Provide rewards and recognition for teams and team members.

Managerial Responsibilities

Establish and approve division-wide quality/productivity policy.

Provide high-level visibility, leadership, and direction to the Quality/Productivity Improvement Program.

Review progress of implementation and continuation plans at regularly scheduled meetings.

Ensure that the quality/productivity planning is consistent with the human resource thrust for organizational effectiveness.

Review and approve annual, long range, and strategic plan quality/productivity goals and objectives.

Demonstrate continued commitment to quality/productivity improvement in both action and communications.

Corrective Action Steering Committee Responsibilities

Problem-Solving Teams

Ground Rules for Establishing and Organizing Teams

When Are Problem-Solving Teams Appropriate?

Problem-solving teams can be used for a variety of purposes. However, before forming a team or suggesting the formation of a team it is useful to consider whether a team approach is appropriate to the problem or situation. Often we may find instances in which a problem can best be resolved through individual work. Following are some guidelines and principles which can help you to decide whether or not the use of a problem-solving team is appropriate.

Problem-solving teams *are not* appropriate:

- When one person clearly has greater expertise on the subject than all others.
- When those affected by the decision acknowledge and accept that expertise.
- When there is a "hip pocket solution": The manager or company already knows the "right answer."
- When someone has the subject as part of his or her regular job assignment, and it *wasn't* his or her idea to form the team.
- When no one really cares much about the issue.
- When no important development or learning about others would be served by their involvement.
- When there is no time for discussion.

Problem-solving teams *are* appropriate:

- For gaining new sources of expertise and experience.
- For allowing all of those who feel they know something on the subject to get involved.
- For building consensus on a controversial issue.
- For allowing representatives of those affected by an issue to influence decisions and build commitment to them.
- For tackling a problem no one "owns" by virtue of organizational assignment.
- For allowing more wide-ranging or creative discussions/solutions than available by normal means (e.g., to get an unusual group together).

Choosing a Chair

Every team needs a chairperson. The manager or steering committee who chartered a problem-solving team has the authority to choose a chairperson or leader if they wish, or they may decide to turn this decision over to the team. There are a number of alternative approaches to choosing a chair or leader. These are:

- A rotating chair or leader.
- The most senior member.
- The member who has the most expertise on the problem.
- The member who is or who represents the group most affected by the problem or by the changes that might come about.
- The "natural leader."
- A random draw.

The position of a chair is very influential on how effectively a team will work together. Therefore, much care and consideration should go into selecting the person to fulfill this role. Other criteria which could be considered are:

- Good interpersonal, communication, and analytic skills.
- Leadership ability.
- Respected by others.
- Fair and unbiased.
- Variety of contacts with people in the areas that are affected by or interested in the problem.
- Interest and enthusiasm about the problem being addressed by the problem-solving team.

Early Decisions and Negotiations

The first few meetings of a problem-solving team should be devoted in part to taking care of all the details of the "infrastructure" of the team; that is, deciding everything that will provide the support, structure, and framework within which the team will function. The more of this that can be decided and explicitly agreed to early on in the team's work, the more smoothly the team will run.

Being clear and explicit about such things as the amount of time the team will require, roles in the group, and measures for success are as important for team members as they are to the managers who supervise the problem-solving team. Team members need to know how much time they will have to set aside for the problem-solving team, what their responsibilities will be, and any other important ground rules. Managers supervising problem-solving teams need to know how their work area's resources (people, time, budget) will be affected by the problem-solving team, what their role in the problem-solving team will be, how they will be kept informed of problem-solving team activities, and so on. Thus, it is important that the problem-solving team comes to a clear agreement on these issues early on in the game, both among the team members and with the manager, group, or steering committee who is supervising them. (There is more on negotiating with management later in this section.)

The following are the types of issues which the team should decide and agree on within the first two or three meetings of the problem-solving team:

- The likely duration of the project.
- The number of meetings required.
- The frequency of meetings.
- The amount of out-of-meeting time required for each member.
- Different phases of the project (e.g., problem specification, information gathering, analysis, recommendation).
- Other people or groups who should be involved or contacted.
- The type of interaction and cooperation needed from other people and groups (see *Stakeholder Analysis,* page 102).
- Budget needed for data gathering and analysis.
- Types of data and information needed and from whom.
- Roles of group members:
  - Who takes minutes.
  - Who arranges meetings.
  - Who sets up meeting room.
  - Who communicates with management and others.
- Milestones for the accomplishments of different stages.
- Measurements for progress and success.
- Reporting requirements to the appropriate manager or group.

Ongoing Coordination with Management

In addition to working with your manager or steering committee early in the process to negotiate relevant issues, it is important to coordinate closely with management *throughout* the course of your work together as a team. Management support is critical for both the ongoing work of the team in terms of providing the resources, legitimacy, and guidance that the team needs, but also in the end when your hard-sought recommendations are received and, hopefully, accepted. The best way to ensure a good supportive relationship with management is to coordinate the work of the team closely throughout the process.

Sometimes during the course of carefully examining a problem, a team may develop a fairly new vision of what the true problem is which can be far afield from the original conception. In other cases, the team may find other issues that had previously been agreed to by management — such as the research methodology, the amount of time required to solve the problem, or the range of possible solutions — may change radically on closer examination. In these instances it is important to meet with management to discuss the new direction and to draw up a new "contract" to ensure that they are in agreement with these new ground rules before you continue.

The more information you can provide management about the purpose, needs, and progress of the problem-solving team, the greater will be management's interest in the team and its ability to support your work effectively. Thus, in addition to fulfilling the formal reporting requirements it would be wise to try to communicate as much as possible to management without, of course, sacrificing the independence of the problem-solving team.

The range of ways that the team could expand its contact and coordination with management include:

- Invite managers to key or critical meetings.
- Provide management with the minutes of problem-solving team meetings.
- Arrange for periodic special meetings with management to inform them on problem-solving team progress and the type of support you could use.
- Ask management to sit in on part of your meetings.
- Assign one problem-solving team member to meet informally with management on a periodic basis.

Meetings: When, Where, and How Often

The three major questions about meetings that your team will have to decide are when, where, and how often to meet? The answers to each of the questions will be contingent on the composition of the team, the location of members, and the importance and complexity of the problem being addressed. All of these issues may be fairly self-evident and easy to resolve; however, here are some guidelines that may assist your team.

There are four major considerations in determining *where* to hold problem-solving team meetings. The location and room should be:

- A place that is convenient for the majority of the members.
- Available to the team for all or most of the time needed so that the team can meet in a familiar place.
- Large enough to accommodate a few extra participants when necessary and whatever materials (audiovisual and flip charts) are needed.
- Small enough to encourage people to sit in a small circle or in close proximity, and to facilitate everyone's participation.

In order to encourage a sense of group coherence, it is best to meet in the same room, rather than shifting spaces.

In general, the following guidelines can be used to determine how often a problem-solving team should meet:

- Frequently in the beginning when much of the work requires the entire group (e.g., defining the problem, setting objectives, planning, etc.).
- Frequently thereafter, if most of the project requires group analysis and decision making.
- Biweekly, if individuals must work independently on parts of the project and then present material for the entire group to consider.

Other factors that could influence your decisions are the following:

- The importance of solving the problem quickly.
- Other competing work and its priority.
- The impact, or lack thereof, of producing results quickly.
- The ability of other people or groups who will be involved in different parts of the project to produce the work required in a given time frame.

Stakeholder Analysis

Many good ideas for changes fail because the interests and needs of affected or interested people and groups were ignored or unknown when the ideas were being formulated. Thus, it is important to take the time early in the problem-solving process to examine carefully the question of which people and groups might be interested in or affected by the current problem and by any changes that the team recommends. Hopefully, all of those parties who have a serious stake in the outcome of the team's work will have been represented by a member in the team. However, there may be others who are more indirectly affected and this analysis is designed to help you to determine who they are and what their interests might be.

There are six steps involved in a stakeholder analysis. These steps are:

1. Identify the current problem and the change desired.
2. Chart all those who are affected by the problem or would have a stake in the changes that might occur:
   - Peers.
   - Supervisors, etc.
3. Determine for each stakeholder:
   - Size of stakes.
   - Criticality of his or her cooperation to the success and acceptance of the change:
     - Necessary
     - Desirable
     - Unnecessary
   - Impact of change on the stakeholders:
     - Power
     - Status
     - Rewards
     - Bosses
     - Knowledge
     - Recognition/visibility
   - His or her critical needs.
   - The resources he or she controls.

4. Inventory your team's resources — power, knowledge, budget, expertise, etc.
5. For each stakeholder whose cooperation is necessary, determine what you can offer/provide that he or she needs in exchange for what he or she has that you want.
6. In addition, try to talk with a representative of each stakeholder group to verify your perceptions of the stakeholder groups' interests and to determine if there is any room for negotiation in terms of reshaping the concept of the problem or the proposed recommmendations.

You can use the form shown in Table 3.1 to conduct a stakeholder analysis.

Stakeholders	Size of Stakes	Need Cooperation?	Impact on Them	Critical Needs	Their Resources	Our Resources	What to Offer
			power ___ status ___ rewards ___ bosses ___ knowledge ___ recognition ___				

Table 3.1 Form for Conducting Stakeholder Analysis
(Copyright © 1983 Goodmeasure, Inc. Cambridge, MA. All rights reserved.)

102

What to Do if Cooperation with Another Area is Required

Many of the problems problem-solving teams address will have components directly or indirectly affecting people or groups outside of your own area. When there is a considerable amount of overlap, the team should probably be composed of representatives from each of the areas and it should be chartered and supervised by a Corrective Action Steering Committee or a group of appropriate managers. In most cases, however, it will not be necessary to extend the composition of the team to include others outside of your area. More likely, your team will need another area to cooperate by providing information that you need reviewing your analysis, or performing some other auxiliary service.

The first step to take when you discover that your team may need some sort of cooperation from another area is to specify clearly exactly what form of cooperation is needed. This might include the following:

- Participating actively during some phase of the project.
- Producing data or information.
- Performing analysis of data.
- Reviewing problem-solving team information or analysis.
- Designing a solution.

The second step is to identify the amount of time and effort that will be needed for the area or person to fulfill its role for the problem-solving team. Just as the problem-solving team needs to negotiate a contract of sorts with its manager about the time and resources the problem-solving team requires, the team should let the other area know what would be required of it. By clearly specifying your requirements in advance you will greatly increase the chance that you will get the results you desire. The team should specify such factors as:

- Amount of time required.
- Persons likely to be involved.
- Data processing requirements.
- Deadlines.

The next step is to inform the manager who is supervising the team that the team requires cooperation from another area. He or she may either give the team the responsibility for approaching the other area directly or may choose to approach the manager of the area personally to request its cooperation. Gaining cooperation from other areas can often prove problematic: They have their own worries and priorities. A manager can be extremely valuable in providing the extra leverage you need to gain this cooperation.

Another approach a team can take is to think about the kinds of services you can offer the work area in a sort of trade for its cooperation. While this may not always be possible or even necessary, the team may find that creative horse-trading can obtain cooperation which otherwise would have been difficult or impossible to obtain.

Gathering Support for the Team's Recommendations

In addition to preparing a good presentation, the team can do a number of other things to lay the groundwork for the acceptance of the team's recommendations to management. One of the most critical issues in gaining acceptance for the recommendation is whether it will be accepted and supported by a wide base of interested parties: your peers, others affected by the change, higher management, etc. The manager or managers to whom the team's recommendations are presented will be considering not only the merits of the idea, but whether it will draw widespread support. Thus, the team can greatly increase the chances of having its recommendaiton adopted if it works hard throughout the process, but particularly at the end before approaching management, to gain support for the proposed changes. This may entail making some revisions in the idea to accommodate the needs of an important person or group. However, these revisions generally serve to improve the recommendation rather than constrain or dilute it.

The following are some guidelines on how to gather support for the team's recommendations. Remember, it is best to seek input and support actively throughout the course of the team's work, and not just at the last minute.

- Seek many inputs. Listen actively to a number of points of view. Then incorporate aspects of each of them into the recommendations and show people exactly where their perspective or suggestion appears.
- Do your homework. Be thoroughly prepared for all meetings and individual discussions. Gather as much hard data as possible and speak knowledgeably from a broad information base.
- Meet with people personally to introduce the team and the proposed recommendation for the first time. It is a good idea to touch base with people individually before any key meetings, and to give them advance warning of what you and others are planning to say at the meeting. Then they can be prepared and coached in the team's point of view.
- Meet with people face-to-face if you expect opposition or criticism. Never gather all potential critics in one room, hoping to hold one meeting to brief everyone. That only helps them discover each other and coalesce as a group. Instead, meet with them individually on their territory.
- Arm key executives with materials and/or rehearse them for any meetings in which questions about your project will come up. Remember that selling others is a two-step process: You are convincing them to back you because you are giving them the tools for selling their *own* bosses or constituencies.
- Make recommendations as specific as possible. A good general rule is to wait until you have tested the idea elsewhere and refined your vague notions before approaching high-level people. The higher the official, the more valuable and scarce is his or her time, and the more focused your meeting has to be. Use peers and subordinates for initial broad

discussions, then focus on specific concrete requests of top executives who want you to quickly get to explaining, "What do you want me to do?"

- Show that the team can deliver. People want to back winners. Early in the process, provide evidence — guarantees, if possible — that the proposed recommendation will work. Later, prove that the team can deliver by meeting deadlines, doing what it promised, etc.
- Indicate the team's willingness to try to get something for supporters that the *supporters* want or need in exchange for their backing: their own pet idea, a piece of a problem situation fixed, access to higher management, credit and visibility, etc. Do creative "horse-trading." Get something from one part of the organization that the team can give to another part in exchange for its support and participation.
- Share credit and recognition. As one successful, innovative manager put it, "Make everyone a hero." If others outside of the team have made valuable contributions, let them and other people know it.

Accountability for Problem-Solving Teams

Problem-solving teams are not independent decision-making or recommending bodies. They are managed and held accountable in much the same way that any other project or routine operation is. While it is up to each manager or supervisory group, such as a steering committee, to design and negotiate the exact nature of the accountability arrangement with problem-solving teams, the basic elements will remain the same in every case.

To Whom is a Team Accountable?
- *Formally,* to the organizational person or persons that chartered the team. This could be the problem-solving team members' manager, if they are all from one work area and the work affects only their area. It could also be a Corrective Action Steering Committee or a team of managers if the problem crosses organizational lines.
- *Informally,* problem-solving teams should keep all interested parties informed of their progress and results.

How Should Teams be Held Accountable?
- The problem-solving team and the person or group supervising it should come to an agreement early in the process about the following:
  - The nature of the problem.
  - The amount of time problem-solving team members will devote each week to the team.
  - The expected duration of the project.
  - The methods to be used to collect data, analyze the problem, and develop recommendations.

- Other resources and support required.
- Interim products and results.
- Reporting requirements.
- Problem-solving teams should submit periodic (monthly) reports in writing or in person on their progress and results to the person or group supervising them.
- The supervisory person or group is responsible for monitoring problem-solving teams' progress and ensuring that they are on track and on schedule.
- The problem-solving team and the supervising group or person should renegotiate the initial agreement whenever it becomes clear that the conditions have or should change.

Who Has the Authority to Make Decisions?

Problem-solving teams are *advisory* groups and should not have the authority to act on the recommendations they have developed. The manager, group, or steering committee that chartered the problem-solving team will consider the proposed recommendations and has the final authority to decide whether to accept or reject the recommendations. In some cases, the manager or group could choose to turn this authority over to the problem-solving team by agreeing to proceed with a problem-solving team's recommendations. Despite this, the manager still remains the ultimate authority to make this decision.

Implementation of Problem-Solving Team Recommendations

Problem-solving teams are not automatically granted authority to oversee the implementation of their recommendations once they have been affected. In fact, implementation may be turned over to other people or groups in many instances. The manager or group of managers who are supervising the team will decide who will be responsible for the implementation of the recommendations.

There are three options with regard to the implementation of problem-solving team recommendations. These are:

1. The problem-solving team may be chartered to oversee the implementation of its recommendations.
2. Implementation may become the responsibility of the relevant manager, managers, or other groups.
3. The problem-solving team may be restructured and then chartered to implement the recommendations.

In cases where the recommended changes will affect several organizational units, several alternative approaches may be taken to implementation. These are:

- The formation of a task force composed of representatives of the affected units will be responsible for implementation.
- The appropriate steering committee could oversee implementation.
- The managers of the affected units could jointly oversee implementation.

- If the pieces of implementation are fairly discrete, the individual units can independently handle the implementation of their pieces.

Communicating with Others in the Organizational Unit

In general, it is good practice, whatever the project or action, to communicate a problem-solving team's progress and results to those with whom the team members work. In many cases, such communication will be unnecessary because the team may be composed of the entire work area and therefore everyone will be well aware of the problem-solving team's work. But whenever this is not the case it would be wise to put a good deal of thought into the various ways and times when you can inform others about what you are accomplishing.

Generally, the problems a problem-solving team addresses will be central to the work and environment of an area and others will be interested in any changes the team is designing. Their cooperation in ultimately implementing, or at least not standing in the way of, the changes the team has recommended will have a significant effect on the successful implementation of the project. One of the best ways to involve people in the changes is to give them as much information as possible at every step of the way about what is in the works. This will also counteract one of the most powerful impediments that the team may face before final acceptance and use of its ideas: fear of the unknown.

Here are some guidelines about when and how to communicate with others about the work and results of the team:

- Inform others at the beginning about the problem the team is addressing.
- As appropriate, ask for input regarding the concept of the problem, its causes, and solutions.
- Inform others along the way of the point at which the team has arrived and any progress thus far.
- Let people know when they can reasonably expect results.
- Inform others as soon as possible about the team's recommendations.
- Fully explain the likely impact of the proposed changes on people's work routines.
- Inform people as soon as possible about the final decision regarding the acceptance by management of the team's recommendations.

There are a variety of vehicles the team can use to communicate with others. Your choice will depend on the type of information you wish to communicate and the "style" to which your area is accustomed. Some means of communication the team could use include:

- Periodic memoranda.
- Problem-solving team newsletter.
- Problem-solving team bulletin board.
- Brief meetings.
- Walking around informally to talk to everyone.
- Formal presentations.

Problem-Solving Teams *Are not* Appropriate:

When one person clearly has greater expertise on the subject than all others.

When those affected by the decision acknowledge and accept that expertise.

When there is a "hip pocket solution": The manager or company already knows the "right answer."

When someone has the subject as part of his or her regular job assignment, and it *wasn't* his or her idea to form the team.

When no one really cares much about the issue.

When no important development or learning about others would be served by their involvement.

When there is no time for discussion.

Problem-Solving Teams *Are* Appropriate:

For gaining new sources of expertise and experience.

For allowing all of those who feel they know something on the subject to get involved.

For building consensus on a controversial issue.

For allowing representatives of those affected by an issue to influence decisions and build commitment to them.

For tackling a problem no one "owns" by virtue of organizational assignment.

For allowing more wide-ranging or creative discussions/solutions than available by normal means (e.g., to get an unusual group together).

When Problem-Solving Teams Are Appropriate

A prospective leader may be chosen by the following traits:

• Good interpersonal, communication, and analytical skills.

• Natural leadership ability.

• Respect of others.

• Fair and unbiased opinions.

• Variety of contacts with people in the areas that are affected by or interested in the problem.

• Interest and enthusiasm about the problem being addressed by the problem-solving team.

Or, prospective leaders may be chosen by one or more of the following methods:

• On a rotating basis.

• By seniority.

• According to expertise.

• According to who represents the group most affected by the problem.

• By random draw.

Criteria for Chair Selection

Negotiation	**Decision**
____ The likely duration of the project	_____
____ The number of meetings required	_____
____ The frequency of meetings	_____
____ The amount of out-of-meeting time required for each member	_____
____ Different phases of the project (e.g., problem specification, information gathering, analysis, recommendation)	_____
____ Other people or groups who should be involved or contacted	_____
____ The type of interaction and cooperation needed from other people and groups (see *Stakeholder Analysis*)	_____
____ Budget needed for data gathering and analysis	_____
____ Types of data and information needed and from whom	_____
____ Roles of group members (e.g., who takes minutes, who arranges meetings, who sets up meeting room, who communicates with management and others)	_____
____ Milestones for the accomplishments of different stages	_____
____ Measurements for progress and success	_____
____ Reporting requirements to the appropriate manager or group	_____

Checklist for Early Decisions and Negotiations

Invite managers to key or critical meetings.

Provide management with the minutes of problem-solving team meetings.

Arrange for periodic special meetings with management to inform them on problem-solving team progress and the type of support you could use.

Ask management to sit in on part of your meetings.

Assign one problem-solving team member to meet informally with management on a periodic basis.

Submit periodic reports.

Coordination with Management

1. Identify the current problem and the change desired.

2. Chart all those who are affected by the problem or would have stake in the changes that might occur:
   - Peers.
   - Supervisors, etc.

3. Determine for each stakeholder:
   - Size of stakes.
   - Criticality of his or her cooperation to the success and acceptance of the change.
     - Necessary
     - Desirable.
     - Unnecessary
   - Impact of change on the stakeholder's:
     - Power
     - Status
     - Bosses
     - Knowledge
     - Recognition/visibility
   - His or her critical needs.
   - The resources he or she controls.

4. Inventory your team's resources — power, knowledge, budget, expertise, etc.

5. For each stakeholder whose cooperation is necessary, determine what you can offer/provide that he or she needs in exchange for what he or she has that you want.

6. In addition, try to talk with a representative of each stakeholder group to verify your perceptions of their interests and to determine if there is any room for negotiation in terms of reshaping the concept of the problem or the proposed recommendations.

Six Steps in Stakeholder Analysis

Seek many inputs.

Do your homework.

Meet with people personally to introduce the team and the proposed recommendation.

Meet with people face-to-face if you expect opposition or criticism.

Arm key executives with materials and/or brief them for any meetings in which questions about your project will come up.

Make recommendations as specific as possible.

Show that the team can deliver.

Indicate the team's willingness to try to get something for supporters that *they* want or need in exchange for their backing.

Share credit and recognition.

Guidelines for Gathering Support for Team Recommendations
(Copyright © 1983 Goodmeasure, Inc. Cambridge, MA. All rights reserved.)

To Whom is a Team Accountable?

- *Formally,* to the organizational person or persons that chartered the team. This could be the problem-solving team members' manager, if they are all from one work area and the work affects only their area. It could also be a Corrective Action Steering Committee or a team of managers, if the problem crosses organizational lines.
- *Informally,* problem-solving teams should keep all interested parties informed of their progress and results.

How Should Teams be Held Accountable?

- The problem-solving team and the person or group supervising them should come to an early agreement about:
  - The nature of the problem
  - The amount of time problem-solving team members will devote each week to the team
  - The expected duration of the project
  - The methods to be used to collect data, analyze the problem, and develop recommendations
  - Other resources and support required
  - Interim products and results
  - Reporting requirements
- Problem-solving teams should submit periodic (monthly) reports in writing or in person on their progress and results to the person or group supervising them.
- The supervisory person or group is responsible for monitoring problem-solving team's progress and ensuring that they are on track and on schedule.
- The problem-solving team and the supervising group or person should renegotiate the initial agreement whenever it becomes clear that the conditions have or should change.

Accountability of Problem-Solving Teams

Inform others at the very beginning about the problem the team is addressing.

As appropriate, ask for input regarding the concept of the problem, its causes and solutions.

Inform others all along the way of the point at which the team has arrived and any progress thus far.

Let people know when they can reasonably expect results.

Inform others as soon as possible about the team's recommendations.

Fully explain the likely impact of the proposed changes on people's work routines.

Inform people as soon as possible about the final decision regarding the acceptance by management of the teams' recommendations.

There are a variety of vehicles which the team can use to communicate with others. Your choice will depend on the type of information that you wish to communicate and the "style" your area is accustomed to. Some means of communication the team could use include:
- Periodic memoranda.
- Problem-solving team newsletter.
- Brief meetings.
- Speaking informally with people.
- Formal presentations.

Guidelines for Communicating Results with Others.

Task Forces in Management:
A Key Development Tool*
(Allan R. Cohen and Barry A. Stein)

One of the standing jokes in organizations is that a camel is a horse designed by a committee. Negative experiences from working in groups have convinced too many people that committees — even when they're called task forces — are just another management trick for delaying action. But managed properly, task forces can be a potent tool both for problem solving and for developing people. As temporary devices, they allow for flexibility — increasingly needed by organizations facing environments that continue to toss up new problems — and provide a potential place for testing, developing, and training people who might otherwise be blocked from the chance to show their talents.

Unfortunately, they are often misused or mishandled, reinforcing the view of task forces as old-fashioned, trivial, or time-wasting nuisances. A better understanding of their potential effectiveness and the problems that can lead to ineffectiveness is therefore important, especially for anyone concerned with the development of promising or unrecognized people. This section will briefly outline some of the ways in which task forces can be managed to increase the payoffs to both organizations and their people.

When Are Task Forces Appropriate?

There are times when organizational problems should be solved by individuals alone:

- When there is one person who clearly has greater expertise on the subject than all others.
- When those affected by the decision acknowledge and accept that expertise.
- When no important development or learning of others would be served by their involvement.
- When there is no time for discussion.

These are stringent conditions. Most of the time, however, a task force or some other form of joint activity is appropriate (Figure 3.1).

The "people development" value of task forces in particular has received too little attention. Task forces can be used very creatively to provide important learning and exposure for organizational members at all levels. To show how task forces can be used better, we need to understand first how organizational arrangements affect behavior. Then we can elaborate on the ways to take advantage of the particular arrangements known as task forces.

---

* Some of the ideas in this section were also presented by Rosabeth Moss Kanter in her keynote address to the NABW Tri-Regional Conference in Milwaukee, in June 1980.

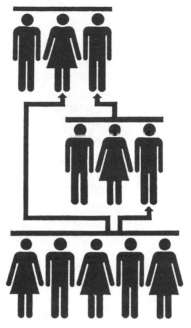

When task forces are useful:

- To gain new sources of expertise and experience.
- To allow representatives of those people or units affected by an issue to influence decisions and to build commitment to them.
- To tackle a problem for which no organizational position is assigned to do it.
- To solve problems affecting many people.
- To allow more wide-ranging discussions/solutions than are likely from the established hierarchy or existing organizational procedures.
- To balance or confront vested interests.
- To address conflicting approaches or views.
- To avoid precipitous action and explore a variety of effects.
- To create an opportunity and enough time to study a problem in depth.
- To develop people through participation and to foster awareness of the issues, add new skills, impart information, and promote valuable contacts.

Figure 3.1 Usefulness of Task Forces

The Impact of Opportunity and Power

Organizations are not merely clusters of people, and effective organizations are not merely clusters of effective people. There are many organizations full of sophisticated, intelligent, and capable people that do not coalesce. There is no coherent philosophy, people do not pull together, and the individuals fail to contribute their skills to overall goals. What is needed, in addition to effective people, is what might be called an "effective structure." Our work with organizations has clearly demonstrated that much of people's response to their work is a response to their environment. In a certain sense, the job makes the person; individuals are seldom able to transcend the circumstances in which they find themselves. To the extent that organizational arrangements make it difficult for people to contribute their talents, they are likely to be less enthusiastic, engaged, or committed than would otherwise be the case.

Specifically, there are two critical characteristics of organizations that shape people's behavior and that are often responsible for underlying effectiveness or the lack of it. These two characteristics are related to the distribution of opportunity, and of power, within the organizations.

Opportunity means not only formal advancement, although that is part of it, but also challenge, growth, and development, the capacity to influence others, and possible progress or growth over a period of time. Thus, opportunity can encompass both situations in which people stay in the "same" job but work on more complex and challenging tasks with increasing rewards, and formal changes in status such as by promotion.

Power means not only authority or the formal trappings that come with a particular position but also the capacity to get the job done, and access to resources that are needed to carry out the organization's work. Power in this sense is equivalent to physical power: Turning on the switch makes the machinery work; turning it off makes the machinery stop. In the same sense organizations need to provide power adequate for people to do their jobs. In the absence of that power people are not likely to do those same jobs well.

Both of these characteristics — opportunity and power — are distributed nonuniformly across organizations. Typically, clerical or secretarial personnel are not in high opportunity positions; that is, they are not expected to grow nor are there career ladders routinely associated with their positions that can promote them or provide challenge above and beyond a traditional range. Contrast that with an entry management position that is conceived as the beginning of a track that in principle can bring people to the top of the corporation, that will continue to open up new avenues, and engage people in a variety of opportunities to contribute. Similarly, some positions provide more access to power than others. People who are in those positions can use whatever personal skills they have more effectively than when they are in positions without any access to power. Thus, whether or not people are in positions with opportunity and power makes a significant difference in their performance, quite apart from their individual talents.

Both opportunity and power have enormous impact on people's effectiveness, self-image, probability of contributing, and capacity to use their latent skills. Specifically, positions high in opportunity are likely to increase occupants' ambition, willingness to take risks, commitment and motivation at work, and the probability of tackling problems that they face. People in positions lacking opportunity tend to be low in ambition, tuned-out, unlikely to take risks, and passive footdraggers rather than committed problem-solvers.

Similarly, people in positions high in power tend to be good leaders; it is much easier to lead people effectively given credibility, clout, and access to broad influence. And, of course, people with power in the sense of access to resources are, by definition, more likely to be effective in carrying out even their individual tasks, whether they are managers or not.

People low in power — that is, people in positions low in power — are likely to be controlling, rules-minded, and overly possessive of their territory. They appear as petty bureaucrats who are often seen as having too much power for their own good. Actually, such people usually have too *little* power. It is powerlessness that corrupts in organizations more than power itself, since those that have too little of it to get cooperation or to be effective cling too tightly to what they have.

Moreover, those subject to negative stereotypes about managerial potential or competence (as in the "bossy woman boss" or the "shiftless and lazy minority person") often are suffering from low power or opportunity rather than individual incompetence. These factors help explain the prevalence and strength of those stereotypes. The stereotypes are a reflection of the fact that such situations have traditionally been characteristics of women and members of minority groups. But the evidence shows clearly that white males in similar positions behave in exactly the same ways. To use available talent fully, organizations need to expand the pool of opportunity and power available to all of their members.

Task Forces to Increase Opportunity and Power

A particularly useful way to increase opportunity and power involves the use of task forces. From this point of view, they are temporary, flexible mechanisms that can provide people with opportunity and power above that in their jobs. In particular, since everyone cannot be promoted (and since some people prefer *not* to be promoted), it is necessary to find ways to add at least some opportunity and power to jobs that in other aspects may be highly routinized or "stuck." This can be done by offering people a chance to participate in such mechanisms as task forces. Thus, the use of task forces provides an important development avenue for managers.

Task forces, after all, first and foremost permit people who aren't normally involved in a given activity to contribute to it. If it's important and highly relevant to the organization's present needs (a key to access of power in general), task forces give more people access to power and greater contribution. If people have little opportunity in their normal assignment, a task force can provide increased challenge, a way to grow and develop, recognition for special skills, and new connections within the organization. All this can help them be seen as more valuable.

Moreover, task forces provide learning opportunities; they offer the chance for people to learn not only about other organizational issues and tasks, but to meet new people, develop important relationships, see how their own work contributes, and develop the skills that enable them to make new contributions in many areas. Thus, task force participation can be rewarding in its own right if certain guidelines are met. It is equally important that the organization view task forces as devices for development as well as for problem solving and that appropriate mechanisms are installed. These considerations lead to a set of "rules" for using task forces effectively.

The Effective Use of Task Forces

To use task forces in a way that brings about these desirable outcomes requires answers to several questions. Depending on the quality of the answers, task forces will be more or less effective and more or less able to engage people usefully.

Which tasks are amenable to a task force approach?

As noted, task forces are not always appropriate. In many organizations task forces are traditionally used only for relatively high-level, important, and new issues. However, they can also be used at much lower levels or in dealing with problems that do not involve large-scale planning. For example, a group of first-line supervisors could effectively join a task force to decide on more effective ways to use clerical help; clerical workers themselves could participate in a task force on ways to get more or better clerical help when it is in short supply.

Many of an organization's questions and tasks are simply handed over to a particular office or role without asking whether or not that is appropriate. Just because the organization has a personnel office, for example, resolution of a company's problems in retaining women might be better achieved by a heterogeneous task force than by assignment to the personnel office or the affirmative action office, though they should obviously be involved. But as indicated earlier, in some situations a task force would be quite inappropriate. The prime examples are tasks that are highly innovative, or that require distinctive, specialized, and new ways of attacking things.

However, it is *not* true that task forces cannot be innovative. Indeed, they are often able to shed old ways of thinking. Even if individuals develop the new ideas, such individuals can usefully join together later in a task force to begin to think through the innovation's implications and to plan implementation. In general, highly routinized tasks do not need task forces, unless problems are resulting from existing operations.

Which people ought to be involved?

Often organizations routinely assign the same people to every task force. If John has done a good job in the past, and top management knows he can be counted on, he's a likely choice for another important task force. But this is backwards; for John, a task force is not a new opportunity but another routine that he has to add to his busy schedule. He is therefore less likely to be committed and to learn. On the other hand, for people who have not ordinarily had that chance, the new opportunity offered by a task force will be an engaging and learning experience. Task forces ought not to be an excuse to give the same people the same set of rewards, as in the classic example of banks that tend to give loans to people who don't need them. Rather, they should be used as a mechanism that can engage new people who have something extra to contribute.

The comparison of a task force ought to be conceived in terms of people who either have something to contribute or who have a potential stake in the outcome. Thus, it makes a great deal of sense for clerical or secretarial people to be on a task force, even if generally composed of much higher level people, if it concerns problems of clerical personnel. Similarly, if the task force decides not to write a report, but rather to present it in person (often a good idea), it might include among the presenters some lower level people for whom that opportunity would not normally exist. There is much evidence that mixed levels in a task force can be enormously effective if given the right support and access to the right resources.

How ought the task force be set up and how ought it function?

Often there is an assumption that a task force calls for a routine or fixed way of dealing with things — a certain number of people are brought together, it always meets after work on Friday for six weeks, and the end result is always a report. This is too limiting. One of the reasons for task forces is their potential to be highly varied in format and operation. People can participate for a small fraction of their time or a large amount. Task forces can work for a few days (indeed, or a single meeting) or remain over a period of a year or more. Task forces can change their membership over time; they need not be fixed. And the time, place, and other arrangements should be tailored to fit the circumstances. This makes it possible for different people to participate, and for the ongoing tasks of the organization to be accommodated more appropriately.

What support and resources are available to the task force and its members?

Does the task force have the resources it needs to do its job, such as time, a budget, access to people, and legitimacy? Or is it supposed to be essentially a fringe activity that members have to "fit in" around the edges? Under the latter circumstances, it's unlikely there will be much enthusiasm or important results. It is particularly here that task forces can be used to empower people, and to provide genuine resources and connections to influential persons who can help see that the conclusions or recommendations are really heard.

The task force's mandate and authority should also be clarified in advance. Is the group supposed to study the problem, develop alternatives for management to choose from, and make recommendations, or make and implement decisions? Whenever possible, and within specified limits, task forces should be empowered to decide. But where that isn't possible, the expectations should be made clear. In one company, a high-level task force studied a contemplated move of corporate headquarters for six months. When its thoughtful and unanimous recommendations were totally rejected — without comment — and another set implemented, it triggered a wave of resentment and anger that still exists.

How can members be given sufficient information to participate effectively?

Participation is not a panacea, and it can have massive dysfunctional results. One of the things learned over the years is that if a group of people from different organizational levels is brought together, some will prove to be much more effective than others. Though it is important to give lower level people a chance to serve, people who do not know how to contribute or who lack basic information about the subjects under discussion will feel frustrated, angry, and ultimately rejected.

It takes time, knowledge, skill, and appropriate information to be able to participate effectively. Thus, organizations that wish to take advantage of task forces to help increase people's opportunity and power need to provide access to training, skills, and background knowledge. Under those circumstances, people from different levels can work together effectively. The wider benefits to the organization are then potentially very great.

How can freedom be balanced with structure?

Occasionally there is an assumption that task forces ought to be completely unfettered, that there ought to be no ground rules or conditions because that limits innovation and constrains outcomes. But this notion does not even apply to brainstorming, which is as near to it as one can get. Even there, careful ground rules and conditions are essential. Not only is structure not harmful, it is necessary. To bring about the possible results, task forces call for careful thought about the structure and arrangement of the group itself. Who will chair meetings? How will the agenda items be determined? Will there be occasional long meetings to work through issues? How will decisions be made? And the answers need to take the particular circumstances into account. (Of course, the task force itself can deal effectively with these questions.)

Is it collaboration or competition?

Task forces are groups, and like any other group, ongoing processes are sometimes helpful and sometimes difficult. In groups, some people are able to be more effective because of the combination of their personal skills and their past experience. Others are less able to be effective. This generates rivalries and jealousies. Similarly, subgroups may form that make it more difficult to achieve a consensus. There may be competition of all sorts. Members may feel more loyalty to their back-home group than to the task force, and they stall to avoid having to "give up benefits" for their home department. Here, the best approach is to anticipate such issues, provide guidance and training to participants if they lack the experience, and provide facilitators where appropriate. Above all, recognize that unless these issues are dealt with straightforwardly, the task force may be less effective than desired, and participants may be upset rather than stimulated.

Every work group needs to examine its functioning periodically, particularly when its processes seem to be preventing effective work. Yet groups often think they can save time by forcing their way when things are divisive or stalled. This is particularly true of task forces, which by definition have limited lives. In general, it is better to stop and discuss *how* the group is functioning than to keep trying to discuss the usual topics. An outside facilitator — from another part of the company, if not an outsider — can often be helpful in breaking log jams and gaining member commitment to make the task force effective. The facilitator, however, cannot be anyone who takes — or is perceived as taking — a partisan position on the issues.

Sometimes task forces must address issues whose resolution will dramatically affect members' home departments. In such cases, there may not be any progress until members form attachments to one another and develop mutual respect. In such cases, long meetings at which "little is apparently accomplished" may be *necessary* to lay the groundwork for results.

Conclusions

Task forces can be useful if managed well. If not, they can be just as tedious as any other mechanism. However, if management thoughtfully considers the questions raised above, it is possible for task forces to serve as flexible problem-solving groups. These can be an extremely powerful tool for people at every level of the organization and for the organization itself. This is, so to speak, a way to put new wine in old bottles.

For individuals joining task forces (rather than creating or managing them), there are some ways to be particularly helpful. First, remember that a major reason for being there is to demonstrate your abilities to others. One good way to do this is to do your homework between meetings. Since others may perceive membership only as a burden, preparing for meetings allows excellent opportunities to demonstrate reasoning or analytic and strategic skills while influencing task force outcomes. Second, take the opportunity to help others, especially higher level people, notice and feel connected to or supportive of you. Use the time to build new relationships, gather information, and generate future supporters. Finally, remember that membership on a task force is like having a license to learn. Don't miss the opportunity to enhance your expertise and perspective.

Under these circumstances every task force has a powerful potential for payoff. Managers who regard task forces only as places where camels instead of horses are produced will be missing an important opportunity for themselves.

Dilemmas of Participation and Teamwork*
(Rosabeth Moss Kanter)

At first glance, teamwork and participation appear to be panaceas and relatively simple to establish and manage. However, there are many paradoxes, dilemmas, and costs as well as benefits associated with teamwork. It will be helpful for both the members of problem-solving teams as well as those who manage and supervise the teams to understand these dilemmas and, hopefully, to strike the best balance between the many trade-offs they will face.

Dilemmas About Beginning

Participation by Command: The Paradox of Initiation

In major organizations, participative activities frequently are initiated because someone at a high level directs others to get involved in task forces, to set up teams, or to treat their subordinates in a different way — and sometimes tells them, in addition, that they will be measured on how well they do this. In short, lower level employees are to be given a greater voice, but their managers — who will be rewarded or punished for implementing such activities — have little say. It certainly looks as though the top leaders are not modeling the behavior they want others to adopt.

But how else can participation be launched? Someone has to initiate the change, and it is hard to prevent at least some others from feeling that participation has been imposed. The irony of participation by command will eventually fade into historical memory as participation is seized and owned by those engaged in it — as long as a second dilemma of initiation is handled well.

"Participate or Else": The Question of Voluntarism

Another issue in launching participation is *which* people get involved, and *how*. Must participation be obligatory, if not mandatory, in order to deserve the label? That is, must everyone be included? Or does participation by definition require volunteers? Can people choose not to participate or to abdicate their decision-making rights to others such as representatives, leaders, or managers? Or should participation be a matter of interest in the issue and the willingness to volunteer? There is a clear dilemma here: If participation relies on volunteers, it is not representative; if it does not, it is coercive.

The question of whether participation is voluntary is always tricky. On the one hand, it is important to handpick people with the skills and enthusiasm for carrying out the activities scheduled for the teams or task forces. On the other hand, it is equally important to avoid making participation simply another "job" to which people are assigned without having any say in the decision.

---

* Adapted from Chapter 10 of *The Change Masters: Innovation for Productivity in the American Corporation* by Rosabeth Moss Kanter. New York: Simon & Schuster, 1983.

Even if the official "rule" for participative activities is "volunteers only," informal pressures can arise that make participation mandatory *de facto* if not *de jure*. What happens if those involved get differentially rewarded because of greater visibility or access to information? What if nonparticipants in task forces get labeled as nonteam players because they turn down the opportunity? Thus, it is also important to avoid the kind of peer and management pressure that make it difficult for someone to say no even if they are asked formally whether they want to get involved. *Balance* is important here.

Dilemmas of Structure and Management

"Escape from Freedom": The Need for Structure
True "freedom" is not the absence of structure — letting the employees go off and do whatever they want — but rather a clear structure that enables people to work within established boundaries in an autonomous and creative way. It is important to establish the ground rules and boundary conditions under which people are working from the beginning: What can they decide? What can't they decide? Without structure, groups often flounder unproductively, so everyone concludes they are merely wasting their time. The fewer the constraints placed on a team, the more time will be spent defining its structure rather than carrying out its task.

Total freedom, with no limits set, is not probable in a business organization in any case; but the limits can be vague, unclear, contradictory, hidden, and subject to guesswork. Accordingly, the group might make a great many false starts before it finally learns what is permissible and what is not. It might spend most of its time discussing how to decide rather than actually making the decision. Too many choices and too much up for grabs can be frustrating. Anchors, that is, something to bounce off of, some constraints or criteria or goals, are necessary.

Delegation Does not Equal Abdication
Related to the structure issue is a key lesson for managers: Delegating responsibility to other people does not mean abdicating managerial responsibilities for monitoring and supporting the process. Some managers assume an either/or world in which they either are in complete control or have given up all control. But delegation — whether of a management team to a set of employee teams or of a single manager to his or her subordinates — means that the manager not only sets the basic conditions, but also stays involved and available to support employees, review results, and redirect or reorient the team as necessary. Leaders can also help coordinate activities, centralize recordkeeping, and serve as points of contact with other departments. Sometimes, of course, a manager who simply wants to prove that participation doesn't work will throw a task at an unprepared team and abdicate all responsibility, thereby setting the whole thing up for failure.

"Who Cares?": Reporting and Accountability
One reason that managers should stay involved, even when delegating responsibility in a participative fashion, is that — ironic though it may seem — the

manager's personal concern for results is a sign of caring to team members. If, having launched it, the manager or the initiator of a team simply walks away from the process and never asks for reports or monitors and measures output, the team members begin to wonder whether this is indeed a high-priority use of their time. They wonder whether anybody really cares about it. But clear accountabilities and reporting relationships are a way of indicating to employees exactly who does care and exactly what value is placed on their activities.

The Twenty-Five-Hour Day Problem

The last issue of concern in launching participation is to find and manage time. Participation in teams and involvement in decisions are time-consuming, and they take time in addition to core jobs. Time is a finite resource. Where will the time come from? Will participation be on company time or employee time? If on company time, is it off the budget of the particular manager or is it compensated in another way? Members or workers may not feel that the extra time they must invest in meetings and in keeping themselves informed is worth the effort, particularly if they feel inadequately paid for the extra time.

Dilemmas of Teamwork

The Seductiveness of the Hierarchy

Teams pulled together from different external statuses, with the awareness that they will be returning to their original status, may slip into "deference" patterns that give those with higher status more air time and their opinions more weight. They generally are provided with a privileged position in the group. Teams may end up duplicating the organizational hierarchy in miniature: higher status people dominating, lower status people dropping out.

The seductiveness of the hierarchy has both emotional and task-related roots. The principal emotions that make it easier to reproduce the hierarchy than to operate as partners are fear and comfort. The basis for fear is obvious: "Crossing" a powerful figure in a group, even if the purpose of the group is to get diversity of opinions, can make people fear later external retribution. So the lower status people hold back, or feel daring if they contribute. But there is also a comfort factor: It is easier in the beginning to maintain familiar patterns of relationships and interaction than to experiment with the unfamiliar.

"Participators Are Made, not Born": The Knowledge Gap

Effective participators are, to an extent, "made, not born." It takes knowledge and information to contribute effectively to task teams, and this has to come from somewhere. Those people with more information about the matters at hand have an advantage over the others. Often organizational position, with resulting differentials in information access, can create this difference in the team. Wherever there is a knowledge gap that is not closed with information before the team meets, inequalities develop that are often frustrating to the less well-informed group members, and they usually respond by dropping out or failing to appear at meetings.

The Internal Politics of Teams

Declaring a group of people a "team" does not automatically make them into one. A philosophy of teamwork in no way eliminates jockeying for status or internal competition if people bring self-serving interests into a group, or if they have differential stakes in the outcome. There may be different advantages to be gained by pushing particular decisions over others; there may be different benefits to be reaped outside the group by appearing to be a dominant force in it   like ambitious young managers who want to impress the boss with their "leadership" skills. People bring different needs and interests into any kind of group, and these can serve as the origins of team politics. Cooperation and reduced politicking are more likely to occur when team members are participating in the group as individuals rather than as representatives, because they can make individual deals free from the pressures of a "shadow group" symbolically looking over their shoulders.

Beyond the politics of interest maximization, teams are also arenas for the flexing of power muscles in and of themselves. There is often nothing inherently more "democratic" about certain decisions because they were made by teams rather than by individual managers. Teams can turn into oligarchies, with a few dominant people taking over and forcing the othes to fall in line.

Finally, teams become politicized when historic tensions between members are not resolved before the "team" is formed. These tensions can become more important when hostile parties are thrown together and forced to interact, especially if they have to rely on each other for reasonable outcomes.

The Myth of "Team"

The mythology that surrounds the idea of "team" in many organizations holds that differences among members do not exist — because they are now a "team" — and therefore it is not legitimate to acknowledge differences or talk about them. Everyone has to act as if all are sharing equally in the group's operations. While inside the team, they have to pretend that they do not see that some are more able than others, or that the highest level people are dominating, or that the chair is railroading another decision through.

Thus members who feel "out" of the group cannot bring up their concerns because of the myth that everyone is "in." People with less to contribute because they are less informed do not feel comfortable seeking help in getting more information so they can contribute more. Why? Because of the myth that everyone has an equal chance to contribute. At the same time, the dominant participators might feel slightly guilty or uneasy about their absorption of a disproportionate share of air time, so they decide to keep quiet for a meeting or two, thereby depriving the group of speedier motion toward solutions.

"It's Hard to Fire your Friend"

A team that "clicks" often develops close bonds that keep people from being open and honest with each other; they fear hurting each other or departing from norms developed in the group. Thus there are some issues for which "impersonal" third parties or managers need to take responsibility.

Dilemmas of Linking Teams to Their Environments

"You Had to Be There": Problems of Turnover

Team spirit is ineffable; it cannot be reduced to a set of events that can easily be described to someone who did not share the experience, and it cannot mean the same thing in the retelling. Newcomers, latecomers, and outsiders have not shared the group's experiences, and often cannot understand the team members' enthusiasm.

At the least, some team momentum is dissipated whenever there is a need to form new relationships and bring newcomers up to speed. Just as when there are long delays between meetings, the group may start spending more time catching up than advancing on the task. Moreover, the new people may all have new suggestions.

Turnover is a problem for teams not only because experienced people leave, but because new people enter. To make sure that a team does not have to repeat itself constantly, revise early decisions, or find its work suddenly changed, continuity of people is clearly required. But because a team is only a small part of a larger system, its boundaries must of necessity be permeable.

"Suboptimization": Too Much Team Spirit

What if the team works so well that it closes itself off from the rest of the organization? A group can get too involved in its own goals and activities and lose sight of the larger context in which it is operating. For example, the kind of things that can help a group pull together — an off-site retreat to communicate better, a sense of specialness and unique purpose, private language, and working arrangements — can also wall it off from everyone else. "Suboptimization" denotes the process by which a group optimizes its own subgoals but loses sight of the larger goals.

While team spirit is a good thing for the team's operations, the group has to remember its relationship to the larger organization and has to be encouraged to remain open to the outside instead of closing itself off. This is especially important in light of the next dilemma.

Stepping on Toes and Territories: The Problem of Power

There is an even larger question involving the link between a team and the rest of the organization: Power problems arise because there are other constituencies who also feel that they have a stake in the problem with which the team is dealing. The team needs to be linked appropriately to these other parties, hopefully from the beginning. Indeed, those whose legitimate territory involves the issues that are being considered by the team should themselves be included in planning for it or carrying it out. An early task is to identify all the parties with a legitimate stake in the issue and decide how they will be involved as the activities are carried out.

NIH (Not Invented Here): The Problems of Ownership and Transfer

It is a familiar organizational phenomenon that organization units want to do things their own way and are reluctant to adopt somebody else's solution. But the do-it-yourself mentality can conflict with building on the results of a team's efforts. This is less of a problem, of course, if the participants simply constitute a work unit that is solving its own problems, and more of a problem if the team is set up to devise programs and procedures that could be potentially useful elsewhere.

The NIH problem highlights another apparent contradiction of participation in large organizations: Participation appears to suggest developments that fall within the arena for participation, but the realities of time constraints and the division of labor mean that some people are going to receive programs designed by others. Some people are inevitably left out. The same ideas arrived at by high participation may seem so useful to those involved, but may be rejected by others in the organization simply because to them these creative team ideas are imposed givens that they played no role in shaping.

"A Time to Live and a Time to Die"

While it is easy for teams to take on a life of their own, participation needs constant renewal, for the sake of both team members and the organization. Even local work unit teams seem to experience burnout after about 18 months of intense activity. This is a common report from companies experienced with large numbers of quality teams or semiautonomous work teams. Periods of intensity need to alternate with periods of distance to give people the energy to continue; new teams need to form or rev up just as old teams begin to drop out.

Planning for the birth and death of teams is important for the organization's ability to reap the full benefits of participation. Those who are left out of one round of team activity can know that they will be included in the future; those among the "elite" of participators know that they will be remerging with the organizational masses in their regular jobs. Former participants leave behind a legacy of their learning which can be used to train and involve new participants, thus smoothing the passing for the dying and the birth for the neophyte.

Conclusions: The Need for Balance

Participation appears to work best when it is well managed and when there is:

- Assignment of meaningful and manageable tasks with clear boundaries and parameters.
- A time frame, a set of accountability and reporting relationships, and standards that groups must meet.
- Information and training for participants to help them become effective team members.
- A mechanism for involving all of those with a stake in the issue in order

to avoid the problems of power and to make sure that those who have input or interest have a chance to get involved.

- A mechanism for providing visibility, recognition, and rewards for teams' efforts.
- Clearly understood processes for the formation of teams, their ending, and the transfer of the learning.

It is clear that managing participation is a balancing act: between management control and team opportunity, between getting the work done quickly and giving people a chance to learn, between seeking volunteers and pushing people into it, and between too little team spirit and too much. There are no rules or formulas for makng participation work that substitute for the sensitive judgment of leaders about how to make the right trade-offs.

Conducting Meetings and Discussions

How to Run Effective Meetings

Much of this section is designed to assist problem-solving teams in holding effective meetings. This section presents an overview of the key elements which can help a team function effectively as a group. The section provides tips on how to conduct better meetings, how to be an effective participant, how to conduct group discussions, and how to use brainstorming and the nominal group technique.

Twelve Steps to Better Meetings

Step 1 — Clarity About the Type of Meeting

It is important to decide in advance and inform others about the overall purpose of the meeting so that eveyone will arrive with the same expectations. Types of meetings include:

- Information sharing
- Problem identification and assignment
- Problem solving

Step 2 — Specific Agenda Circulated in Advance

Following the logic of the previous point, a meeting should have a specific agenda to ensure that it is focused and productive. Circulating the agenda in advance gives people a chance to submit recommendations for revisions, if appropriate, and to prepare themselves for the meeting by gathering information, preparing questions, conducting preliminary analyses, and other activities.

Step 3 — Materials Circulated for Advance Preparation

The principle here is that the more team members can read and review the agenda topics in advance, the more effective the team will be during the meeting. How many times have we seen meetings held twice, the second time after participants had a chance to review the material that was distributed during the first meeting? This is a waste of everyone's time.

Step 4 — Specific Agenda Stated at the Outset

It is valuable to start every meeting by restating the agenda to ensure that everyone concurs (or to revise it, if necessary) and to make sure that it remains in the forefront of everyone's mind throughout the meeting. With the agenda firmly in mind everyone, not just the chair or the leader, will try to keep the meeting on track.

Step 5 — Clear Leadership

Regardless of how well a group functions together, every group needs a leader to direct and guide it toward the achievement of its objectives. Therefore, it is

131

important that it is clearly understood at the outset of the meeting who will be leading the meeting and exactly what responsibilities they are expected to fulfill.

Step 6 — Clear Definition of Each Issue on the Table, and Staying on Track with Each One

People can have different perceptions about what is under discussion and assume that their understanding is the same as everyone's understanding. The outcome of such a situation is wasted discussion, confusion, and sometimes unnecessary conflict. Spending the time when a new issue is introduced to clarify it and check that everyone is operating under the same assumption is worthwhile.

Step 7 — Recording All Ideas and Noting Issues

Often good ideas and decisions that have been carefully hammered out in a meeting are lost, changed, or forgotten because no record was made of them. The best way to record ideas in a meeting is to use a flip chart or some other visual aid. It is also important to note issues that have been raised which are not directly relevant to the discussion at hand, but which should be dealt with at a later date. The public notation of these issues serves a secondary purpose of helping the meeting stay on track because it reassures the person who raised the important, but currently irrelevant, idea that they will have a hearing at another time.

Step 8 — Response and Recognition for Individuals' Contributions

Providing some sort of response and feedback to everyone's ideas will encourage people to participate in the discussion and make them feel that they are valued members of the team. All this is important for the care and feeding of teams.

Step 9 — Exploration of Alternative Solutions

Don't close the discussion of solutions as soon as one viable solution has been recognized. It may be tempting to save time by stopping as soon as one good solution arises; however, further discussion may reveal several other even better ones. When a reasonable solution has been put on the table, spend a little more time exploring alternative solutions and critiquing the one that has been offered before settling on the final solution.

Step 10 — Checking for Consensus

One of the easiest and most dangerous things that a meeting leader or chair can do is to assume that everyone agrees with one's own perceptions and judgments. The results can be false consensus, passive withdrawal, confusion, and so on. The best way to avoid getting caught in these traps is to take time periodically throughout the meeting and at the end to check for consensus in the team. While you may not always find that consensus exists, it is much better to know that it does not exist than to assume incorrectly that it does. It will be more costly to switch tracks later on when more time and resources have been invested in an approach which was problematic and lacked the full support of key parties.

Step 11 — Identification of Actions: The "Who, What, When" Rule

Once a decision has been reached it is critical to assign a person or group the task of transforming the idea into concrete action. The team should decide *who* will be responsible for acting, *what* that person must do, and *when* this should happen. In many cases, the "what" will be to present the team's recommendations formally to the appropriate manager or group rather than the team itself actually taking action on a decision. The identification of action, in effect, constitutes the team's follow up plan.

Step 12 — Periodic Review and Adjustment of the Agenda

It is not unlikely that new and important agenda items may arise during the course of a meeting. Time should be taken to reassess the agenda and consider revising it in the light of new directions or priorities which have come out during the meeting. The agenda is not etched in stone; it is there to facilitate the discussion of important issues. If the team develops a new sense of the right direction for the meeting, then the agenda should be revised accordingly.

How to Be an Effective Participant in Meetings

Being an effective participant in a meeting is almost as difficult and time-consuming as trying to lead an effective discussion. The responsibility for the effectiveness of any meeting rides as much on the individual participants as it does on the team leader. In fact, a team in which every member understood the importance of his or her role and knew how to participate effectively would scarcely require any leadership at all. It is not enough to voice one's opinions on the subject at hand; there are a variety of other considerations which can significantly affect individual and, ultimately, team performance and effectiveness. None of these issues (see the following checklist) are particularly difficult to act on, but they are the kind of things whose importance we often tend to either forget or underestimate.

Personal Checklist for Participation in Meetings

Am I:

- Exercising discipline by staying with the issue on the table?
- Using paper to note additional thoughts?
- Speaking for myself and not making assumptions about others' views?
- Listening to, recognizing, and rewarding contributions of others?
- Helping to draw out silent members?
- Sharing responsibility for the state of the meeting? For leadership tasks?
- Using "itemized response"? (Here's what I like about that idea. Here are my concerns.)
- Maintaining eye contact with speakers?
- Speaking up if I disagree or have concerns?
- Respecting others by being on time?
- Showing energy, enthusiasm, and a positive outlook?
- Ready to work?

Conducting Group Discussions

Conducting a group discussion is more of an art than a skill; but it is an art that can be learned and one which will greatly benefit the team. Since much of the work which will be accomplished by problem-solving teams will be achieved through group work, the ability to lead group discussions so that they are productive is critical for success. This will be a new skill and requirement for many people, whereas others may be old hands at guiding groups.

There are two key objectives in conducting discussions that must be kept in mind all the time. The first is that the chair or leader must encourage people to share their ideas and opinions. That sounds simplistic, however, we have all been witness at one time or another to meetings where no one spoke up or no one dared to challenge or offer alternatives to the few ideas that were on the table. Unfortunately, it is much easier to kill than encourage free discussion.

The second objective in conducting discussions is to keep them on track, on the subject, and moving toward a conclusion or resolution. Again, this sounds simple, however it is easy to be disrupted by a digressive idea, follow it and other new tangents, and end the meeting with a new set of issues and no progress in resolving the issues for which the meeting was called. The primary cure for this group wandering is to refer back to the agenda and the objectives for the meeting continually, and to ask whether the discussion is on track. Important ideas that have been raised but which are not pertinent to the agenda can be noted and dealt with in another meeting or in some other way.

The following list provides some examples of actions the discussion leader can take to run a lively discussion in which everyone feels free to participate. The list will also provide ways to keep the discussion on track.

- State the agenda at the beginning of the meeting. Ensure that everyone is proceeding with the same understanding about the purpose of the meeting.
- Remain in the background. A good meeting leader will talk no more than 20 percent of the time.
- Refer to the agenda and meeting objectives frequently. Ask whether members think they are sticking to the agenda and whether it is time to move on to another item.
- Prepare questions in advance of the meeting. For example, "How can we make this a better place to work?"
- Stop the discussion of digressive or irrelevant issues. Note these ideas on a flip chart if they are important and assign them to the agenda of another meeting or delegate their resolution to the appropriate person.
- Avoid rehashing the same ideas again.
- Acknowledge decisions and consensus when they occur. By asking for everyone's agreement that an agenda item has been adequately addressed you can move on to another item with less chance of backsliding.

- Brainstorm. Encourage people to contribute many ideas and wait until the idea-generation period is completed before evaluating them.
- Don't directly disagree with a member; ask the group to help in evaluating ideas.
- Draw out differences of opinion. Disagreement can be useful and false consensus will backfire later.
- Ask questions that require more than a "yes-no" answer.
- Don't barrage people with a long series of questions. Give team members a chance to respond to each question.
- Allow silence to occur. If there is silence someone (other than you) will eventually respond.
- Look directly at the person in the group who speaks or whom you have addressed. If you seem to be really interested in hearing what someone has to say, he or she is more likely to want to participate in the discussion.
- Provide ample sign of response to everything that is said through a variety of means:
  - Write it down
  - Rephrase what someone said
  - Ask further questions
  - Make supportive comments
- Use small groups, if necessary. People are sometimes more confident speaking out in a small group. Ask each group to report to the whole group when discussions are completed.

Brainstorming and the Nominal Group Technique

Brainstorming and the Nominal Group Technique provide discussion leaders with a structured means to encourage a team to generate ideas spontaneously. These techniques are particularly useful to encourage the participation of everyone in a meeting, not just the vocal few. These discussion techniques are most appropriately used when a group is trying to generate a range of options or alternatives in problems, causes, and solutions. Other techniques can then be used to assess and evaluate the ideas generated by the brainstorming technique carefully. Brainstorming gets all the ideas out on the table — often a fairly difficult task.

The basic guidelines for brainstorming are simple:
- Allow ample time for listing all of the ideas that the team has to offer.
- Stress *quantity*, not quality of ideas.
- Encourage *each* team member to present whatever ideas he or she believes are important (no matter how ridiculous or unimportant the ideas may seem).
- Prohibit criticism or evaluation of contributions until the brainstorming session is over.

There are three primary brainstorming methods: Round Robin, Free-Wheeling, and Slip. Each has advantages and disadvantages the team or discussion leader will have to weigh before determining which one would best suit the particular characteristics of the team.

In the *Round Robin* method the leader asks each team member in turn to contribute an idea as it relates to the purpose of the discussion. Every idea is recorded on a flip chart by the leader or someone else. When a team member has nothing to contribute, then he or she simply says "pass." The next time around, this person may offer an idea if they wish or pass again. Ideas are solicited until no one has anything to add.

The Round Robin method has a number of advantages. It makes it difficult for any one person to dominate the discussion. Because the discussion is focused on a single issue, it does not get off track. Everyone is given the opportunity to participate fully. The major disadvantage of this method is that people may feel some frustration while they are waiting for their turn.

With the *Free-Wheeling* method team members can call out ideas freely and in a random order. This process continues until no one has anything to add. As with the Round Robin method all ideas are written on a flip chart by someone assigned to the task.

The major advantage of this method is that it is very spontaneous and there are no restrictions whatsoever. The primary disadvantages are that some individuals may dominate the discussion while quiet team members may be reluctant to participate. In addition, it can be chaotic if too many people talk at the same time.

The *Slip* method is quite different from both the other two brainstorming methods. In the Slip method each team member writes down on a piece of paper as many ideas as he or she can think of. Then, the leader collects the slips and writes all the ideas on a flip chart.

The primary advantage of this method is that all contributions remain anonymous, so members who are afraid to express themselves publicly feel freer to contribute their ideas. The primary disadvantage is that some creativity may be lost because members do not hear and react to the contributions of others.

The *Nominal Group Technique* is a refinement of brainstorming. It provides a structured discussion and decision-making technique. Basically, the individuals on a team are asked to respond to a specific task statement with written answers. This is followed by an exploratory discussion. It closes with a prioritization and ranking of the ideas generated.

There are five steps for conducting a Nominal Group Technique session. First, there is an opening introduction in which the purpose of the session and the process to be followed is explained. Participants are then presented a carefully worded *task statement* (the question or issue to be considered). The task statement should be clear, simple, and direct, and everyone should understand the question or issue at hand.

Next, there is a *silent generation* of ideas. Each person, working alone, makes a written list of his or her ideas and responses to the task statement. Normally eight to 10 minutes are allowed for this step, but the time is flexible and the step should last as long as most of the people are generating ideas.

The third step is a Round Robin phase. Participants are asked, one by one, to state one of the responses or ideas they have written. A participant proposes only one item at a time and someone records each item on a flip chart as it is presented. No evaluative discussion of the ideas at this point is allowed. Participants may pass at any time and join in any subsequent round. They are encouraged to add items to their personal list should new ideas occur to them during the Round Robin. This phase goes on until all the ideas generated by the group are listed and displayed.

The fourth step is *clarification*. The leader takes each item one by one, asking if any clarification is necessary to their understanding. Pace is important to this step, and the leader avoids lengthy discussions, arguments, and "speech making." The purpose of this step is to clarify rather than evaluate, and to continue providing opportunities for participation.

Finally, there is the *voting* and *ranking* step. With a short list (less than 14), each person chooses five priority items. For longer lists (more than 40), up to nine priority items are chosen. A check mark is placed next to each item as the members of the group vote. The number of votes per item will then denote the order of priority for each item.

1. Clarity about the type of meeting.

2. Specific agenda circulated in advance.

3. Materials circulated for advance preparation.

4. Specific agenda stated at the outset.

5. Clear leadership.

6. Clear definition of each issue on the table and staying on track with each one.

7. Recording of all ideas and noting new issues.

8. Response and recognition for the individual's contributions.

9. Exploration of alternative solutions.

10. Checking for consensus.

11. Identification of actions: the "who, what, when" rule.

12. Periodic review and adjustment of the agenda.

Guidelines for Conducting Effective Meetings

Am I:

_____ Exercising discipline by staying with the issue on the table?

_____ Using paper to note additional thoughts?

_____ Speaking for myself and not making assumptions about others' views?

_____ Listening to, recognizing, and rewarding contributions of others?

_____ Helping to draw out silent members?

_____ Sharing responsibility for the state of the meeting? For leadership tasks?

_____ Using "itemized response"? (Here's what I like about that idea. Here are my concerns.)

_____ Maintaining eye contact with speakers?

_____ Speaking up if I disagree or have concerns?

_____ Respecting others by being on time?

_____ Showing energy, enthusiasm, and a positive outlook?

_____ Ready to work?

Personal Checklist for Meeting Participation
(Copyright © 1983 Goodmeasure, Inc. Cambridge, MA. All rights reserved.)

State the agenda at the beginning of the meeting. Ensure that everyone is proceeding with the same understanding about the purpose of the meeting.

Remain in the background. A good meeting leader will talk no more than 20 percent of the time.

Refer to the agenda and meeting objectives frequently. Ask whether members think they are sticking to the agenda and whether it is time to move on to another item.

Prepare questions in advance. For example, "How can we make this a better place to work?"

Stop the discussion of divergent or irrelevant issues. Note these ideas on a flip chart if they are important and assign them to the agenda of another meeting or delegate their resolution to the appropriate person.

Avoid rehashing the same ideas again.

Acknowledge decisions and consensus when they occur. By asking for everyone's agreement that an agenda item has been adequately addressed you can move on to another item with less chance of backsliding.

Brainstorm. Encourage people to contribute lots of ideas and hold off evaluating them until the idea-generation period is completed.

Don't directly disagree with a member; ask the group to help in evaluating ideas.

Draw out differences of opinion. Disagreement can be useful and false consensus will backfire at a later point.

Ask questions which require more than a "yes-no" answer.

Don't barrage people with a long series of questions. Give team members a chance to respond to each question.

Allow silence to occur. If there is silence someone (other than you) will eventually respond.

Look directly at the person in the group who speaks or whom you have addressed. If you seem to be really interested in hearing what someone has to say, he or she is more likely to want to participate in the discussion.

Provide ample signs of response to everything that is said through a variety of means:
- Write it down
- Rephrase what someone said
- Ask further questions
- Make supportive comments

Use small groups, if necessary. People are sometimes more confident speaking out in a small group. Ask each group to report to the whole group when discussions are completed.

Guidelines for Conducting Group Discussions

Feedback is information given to another person that helps them learn more about their behavior and its effects on others. What follows are some guidelines that enhance good communication and keep the situation from degenerating into mere name-calling or anger.

Feedback should ideally be:

- **Requested and invited.** At least the person getting feedback should genuinely agree to hear it.

- **Helpful.** It doesn't help to hear about things over which you have no control or which you cannot change. It is most helpful to hear about behavior that could be modified if the person wishes. Similarly, it doesn't help (and nobody likes) to hear advice or second-guessing about how you should have behaved.

- **Appropriate.** Speculation or guessing about the motives behind behavior is not very appropriate. What is appropriate is to stick to a concrete situation.

- **Descriptive.** "What actually happened," or data about events, gestures, and words. Good feedback is information about "what" and "how." It is *not* about "why." It is also not a set of labels ("You are such-and-such a kind of person"), but a statement about actual behavior ("Yesterday you did such-and-such"). A good test of the descriptive quality of feedback is how much it includes of what the person actually did.

- **Specific, concrete, and involving as many details as possible.** These details are critical to help the other person understand what he or she actually *did*.

- **Timely and as close to the actual event as possible.** (And given at the right time, when the other person can really listen to it.) Feedback becomes less and less useful the further away from the actual events. But it also is more effective if the timing is right, and if both parties are ready to communicate in a positive way.

- **Positive as well as negative.** Good feedback includes both sides.

- **Specifically related to the person giving it.** Feedback is never "the truth" — it is only what the other person saw and felt. It helps to put it in this way: "Here's the impact that had on *me*." "When you did such-and-such, it made me uncomfortable." One person can never tell another person what he or she felt or should have done; people can only talk about their own perceptions.

- **Offered with a chance for the receiver to respond.**

- **Able to be tested and confirmed.** Is there a way to get more data and perhaps the reactions of other people? Can the receiver of feedback tell the giver about his or her reactions? Is there more information to be obtained or to be shared?

Feedback is always a two-way process.

How to Give Feedback

Organizational politics are a fact of organizational life that should not be ignored when problem-solving teams are selecting problems to work on, solutions to recommend, or plans for implementation. No matter what the technical or analytic merit of the proposal is, if the team does not also recognize and deal with the stakes and positions of the various people and groups who will be interested in or affected by the proposal they may run into unnecessary roadblocks. Worse still, a strong opponent who has not been dealt with adequately in advance can succeed in killing an excellent project.

The following exercise will help teams to analyze the organizational politics that surround their proposal. It will help to identify your allies and your potential opposition and to think about how to lessen the chances of opposition.

Who recognizes that this is an issue?_____

_____

Who does not yet recognize this issue? _____

_____

What is the organization's stance with respect to this issue? For example:

Ignore	Assign to protectors (staff roles)
Wait and see	Involve/change line operations
Defend	Does the stance seem appropriate

Who has "ownership" — legitimate control over any key aspect of this issue?

_____

_____

What potential outcomes do you see? Who would benefit? Who would lose?

Outcomes	"Beneficiaries"	"Losers"
_____	_____	_____
_____	_____	_____
_____	_____	_____
_____	_____	_____

What is our degree of involvement in this issue?_____

_____

What is our stake in the outcomes?_____

_____

With which potential beneficiaries and losers do we identify? _____

_____

With whom should we ally to improve our position with respect to influencing questions about this issue?

_____

_____

Issue Analysis Exercise

When a team is in the process of choosing a problem to work on (if it is given that discretion) or a solution to recommend, there are many considerations beyond the technical or analytic merit of the idea — the fact that everyone in the team feels that one problem is clearly the *most* important or that one solution stands out as the *best*. In addition to merit, it is important to think about whether the proposal is likely to fly. Does it have a good chance of being accepted and adopted by your organization? Your team will have accomplished little or nothing if their technically perfect recommendation has no chance (for reasons other than merit) of seeing the light of day.

Furthermore, it is even more important to pay attention to these issues when the Corrective Action Process is in its early stages in your organization and is itself still on trial. A series of failed proposals for the selection of problems or for recommendations could undermine the credibility of the process itself. Thus, we present here some of the other factors which could be considered in choosing a problem to work on or a solution. Keeping these in mind should improve the chances that your team's ideas will succeed and that quality and productivity gains will be achieved.

1. *Trial-able*. It can be demonstrated on a pilot basis.
2. *Reversible*. The organization can go back to preproject status if it doesn't work.
3. *Divisible*. It can be done in segments or phases.
4. *Sunk costs*. It is in an area where there are prior resource commitments; it builds on them.
5. *Concrete*. It is concrete rather than abstract and involves tangible results rather than philosophy.
6. *Familiar*. It is consistent with a successful experience with a similar project in the past.
7. *Congruent*. It fits the organization's direction.
8. *Publicity value*. It has visibility potential if it works.
9. *Marginality*. (If the selling job is hard.) It does not challenge system values or procedures and appears off-to-the-sidelines enough that no one will notice that it brings change.
10. *Idiosyncrasy*. (If all else fails.) It is something you can do by yourself, for yourself, under your own power.

Ten Characteristics of Projects "Most Likely to Succeed"
(Source: Goodmeasure's "99 Propositions About Innovation from the Research Literature.")

Seek many inputs. Listen actively to a number of points of view. Then incorporate aspects of each of them into the project plan — and show people exactly where their perspective or suggestion appears.

Do your homework. Be thoroughly prepared for all meetings and individual discussions. Gather as much hard data as possible — all the facts — and speak knowledgeably from a broad information base.

Meet with people one-on-one to first introduce yourself and your idea. It's a good idea to touch base with people individually before any key meetings, and to give them advance warning of what you and others are planning to say at the meeting. Then they can be prepared and coached in your point of view.

Hold one-on-one meetings when you expect opposition or criticism. Never gather all of your potential critics in one room, hoping to hold one meeting to brief everyone. That only helps them discover each other and coalesce as a group. Instead, meet with them individually, on their territory.

Arm relevant key executives with materials and/or rehearse them for meetings in which questions about your project will come up. Remember that selling others is a two-step process: You are convincing them to back you because you are giving them the tools for selling their *own* bosses or constituencies.

Make your requests and your project as specific as possible. A good general rule: Wait to approach high-level people until you have tested the idea elsewhere and refined your vague notions. The higher the official, the more valuable and scarce his or her time, and the more focused your meeting has to be. Use peers and subordinates for initial broad discussions, then focus on specific, concrete requests of top executives who want you to explain quickly, "What do you want me to do?"

Ask for specific rather than broad support. It is easier to get backing for a concrete idea than a general endorsement of anything you might want to do. You reduce the risks for others; they do not have to be in favor of *everything* you have done or everything you stand for in order to support a specific initiative.

Show that you can deliver. People want to back winners. Early on, provide evidence — guarantees, if you can — that this project will work. Later, prove that you can deliver by meeting deadlines, doing what you promised, etc.

Indicate your willingness to get for your supporters something that *they* want or need in exchange for their backing: their own pet idea, a piece of a problem situation fixed, access to higher management, credit and visibility, etc. Do creative "horse-trading": get something from one part of the organization that you can give to another part in exchange for their support and participation.

Share credit and recognition. As one very successful, innovative manager puts it, "Make everyone a hero."

"Selling" Others: How to's for Gathering Support for Projects

PART FOUR
MANAGING TEAMS

Introduction to the Role of Management in Corrective Action

Roles and Responsibilities of Managers in Productivity and Quality Improvement Processes

One of the most misunderstood perceptions about participative leadership (and the main reason for its downfall) is that it equals or sanctions the abdication of management. This is entirely false. Managers are just as important in participative projects such as problem-solving teams as they are in any other part of the business. As we all know, simply designating a group or team and giving them a mandate does not necessarily translate into a successful result. There must still be a lot of careful management involved from the start to the finish to ensure the best possible outcomes. Thus, the role of management is critical to the success of corrective action and a Quality or Productivity Improvement Program as a whole.

Managers who are supervising problem-solving teams also have a set of responsibilities to fulfill. Managers may have full or shared responsibility for supervising a team depending on whether the team is composed entirely of their subordinates or whether the team crosses organizational or work areas. In the latter case, the manager may be sharing responsibility with one or more managers.

Managers have responsibility for the following:

- Deciding how much of the problem can be turned over to a problem-solving team.
- Chartering problem-solving teams.
- Agreeing to release subordinates to join teams crossing organizational lines.
- Setting clear constraints and boundaries as appropriate regarding the problem to be addressed, research methodology, the range of options for solutions, etc.
- Allocating the necessary resources (time, people, budget) to support the team.
- Actively supporting the team in own work area and elsewhere as needed.
- Troubleshooting for the team, especially when it needs cooperation from another area.
- Informing the team about relevant issues and changes in circumstances and the environment.
- Staying involved in and informed about team activities, plans, and progress.

- Reviewing progress and results against the plan regularly.
- Informing others (at all levels) about team activities, plans, and progress.
- Deciding quickly whether or not to accept the team's recommendations.
- Deciding quickly when and how to implement the accepted recommendations.
- Providing rewards and recognition for teams and team members.

Managing Teams and the Process

Establishing Teams and Setting Basic Ground Rules

Problem-solving teams may be formed on a volunteer basis or through assignment. The manager or supervisor who charters a problem-solving team has the discretion to choose the approach. Although most people prefer the volunteer approach because it reinforces a new culture of participation, there are costs and benefits associated with it.

Volunteer Benefits

- Volunteers are more enthusiastic.
- There is no coercion.
- People who really care about the issue will volunteer.

Volunteer Costs

- People who have the necessary expertise and knowledge may not volunteer.
- Too many people may volunteer.
- Too few people will volunteer.

A manager will have to assess the situation he or she is faced with and weigh the likely costs and benefits of using volunteers to decide this issue. Factors such as the following should be considered: (1) people's feelings about the issue of volunteer composition, (2) the number of people in the pool with the requisite knowledge and skill, (3) the likelihood that not enough people will volunteer, and (4) the complexity and importance of the problem to be addressed.

A problem-solving team can only be as good as its individual members. The combined qualities, skills, knowledge, and experience of the team members will determine how successfully the team will be able to resolve the problem they face. Thus, it is critical to spend some time considering the likely requirements for being able to analyze and solve the problem that a problem-solving team will be assigned.

The following guidelines should prove helpful in making this important determination:

- Include people who *have the expertise, knowledge,* and *experience* needed to analyze and solve the problem.
- Include people who *have access to the information* needed to understand, analyze, and solve the problem.
- Include people who *will be affected by the changes* that result from the implementation of the problem-solving team's recommendations.
- Include people who *will be involved in implementing* the changes.

Once you have determined the criteria for selecting team members it will be important to tell people what criteria will be used. Informing people can help to avoid the hurt or angry feelings that sometimes arise when people are not asked to join a special assignment.

Regardless of whether you are using the volunteer or assignment approach to composing a problem-solving team, it is important to pay careful attention to the system you use to make and announce the selection of team members. If done poorly, the process can undermine whatever sense of teamwork your area has developed.

Keep these guidelines in mind when you design a system to select the members of a new problem-solving team.

- If the voluntary approach is used and too many people volunteer:
  - Make sure everyone knows they can volunteer.
  - Make sure people know how they can volunteer.
  - Inform people about the selection process used.
  - Make sure that the selection process is fair and perceived to be fair.
  - Thank those who were not selected for the corrective action team and assure them that they will have the opportunity to participate in another project later.

- If the aproach is not voluntary:
  - Make sure everyone knows that a problem-solving team is forming and what problem will be addressed.
  - Make sure everyone knows the selection criteria.
  - Make sure that the selection process is fair and perceived to be fair.
  - Let those who were not selected, but could have been (i.e., they had similar qualifications to problem-solving team members chosen) know why they were not selected and that there will be opportunities for them to contribute in the future if they wish.

Managers should pay careful attention to setting guidelines and ground rules before the problem-solving team is chartered and at the start-up of the problem-solving team. Setting ground rules is one of the most critical roles managers play in supporting and managing problem-solving teams. If the ground rules are clearly specified, agreed on, and known to all, the likelihood of a successful outcome and a smooth process is much higher. The problem-solving team needs to know exactly what the boundaries, constraints, and rules are by which they are playing. You will want to know these too so that you will not be faced with unpleasant surprises based on misunderstanding and so you are clear about what is expected of you as a manager in this process.

Before you charter a problem-solving team to address a problem it is important to spend some time clarifying the exact nature of the problem and the parts of the problem which will be open to analysis. In many cases, there may be aspects of a problem that can only be decided by management or that may already have been determined. The problem-solving team needs to know the boundaries of its work so it does not end up going down a path only to discover that that part of the problem has already been solved or that they are stepping on someone else's toes.

Similarly, managers should be clear about possible solutions to a problem that have already been rejected. One of the most devastating things that can happen to a team is to present its hard work through a solution to management only to be told that it had been rejected in the past or for some reason could not be considered among the set of possible options. Being explicit about constraints at the outset will help you to avoid these pitfalls.

The first few meetings of a problem-solving team will be devoted in part to deciding the problem-solving team's position on all the details of how members will work together. It is important for you to consider your own position on these issues so that you will be knowledgeable when you meet with the problem-solving team to agree on the ground rules. Among the issues which you should consider are:

- The likely duration of the project.
- The number of meetings required.
- The frequency of meetings.
- The overall allocation of people resources.
- Different phases of the project (e.g., problem specification, information gathering, analysis, and recommendation).
- Types of cooperation needed from other people and groups.
- Budget available for data and analysis.
- A schedule for the completion of the work.
- Measurement for progress and success.
- Reporting requirements.

You may find that circumstances change during the period a problem-solving team is working on a problem and that these affect some of the ground rules to which you have agreed. For example, an option that had formerly been excluded from the set which the problem-solving team could pursue may for some reason be found to be acceptable. In such cases, you should inform the problem-solving team as soon as possible of the changes in the ground rules.

Include people who *have the expertise, knowledge, and experience* needed to analyze and solve the problem.

Include people who *have access to the information* needed to understand, analyze, and solve the problem.

Include people who *will be affected by the changes* that result from the implementation of the problem-solving team's recommendations.

Include people who *will be involved in implementing* the changes.

Volunteer Benefits

- Volunteers are more enthusiastic.
- There is no coercion.
- People who really care about the issue will volunteer.

Volunteer Costs

- People who have the necessary expertise and knowledge may not volunteer.
- Too many people may volunteer.
- Too few people may volunteer.

Choosing Team Members
(Copyright © 1983 Goodmeasure, Inc. Cambridge, MA. All rights reserved.)

The likely duration of the project _____

The number of meetings required _____

The frequency of meetings _____

The overall allocation of people resources _____

Different phases of the project (e.g., problem specification, information gathering, analysis, and recommendation) _____

Types of cooperation needed from other people and groups ____

Budget available for data and analysis _____

A schedule for the completion of the work _____

Measurement for progress and success _____

Reporting requirements _____

Ground Rules: What Teams Need to Know at the First Meeting

Managing Teams: The Later Stages

A manager has two primary responsibilities to fulfill once a problem-solving team is up and running: to carefully monitor the team's progress and to decide whether to accept or reject the team's recommendations. In this section these two responsibilities will be discussed briefly.

Monitoring Teams

Monitoring a problem-solving team's progress is one of the manager's primary responsibilities in the Quality/Productivity Improvement Process. Since the idea of having relatively autonomous work teams participate in the problem solving and implementation may be quite new in your organization, it is important that you not abdicate your managerial responsibilities. Participative management is never permissive management, and one of your key tasks will be to keep an open channel of information flowing both to and from the problem-solving teams.

Teams should be tracked and monitored by managers just as closely as managers monitor any other activities, functions, or projects. While it is important that you not intervene at every possible moment, you do have a "right to know" about the activities and progress of the team.

Close monitoring provides credence to the idea that the problem the team is attempting to solve is important to the organization — your attention can be a measure of that. It is a way of sending a clear message that their work is considered to be critical by management. This will also help to keep the momentum going on the problem-solving team — to know that you will expect regular reports and progress. You may also consider monitoring to have a developmental aspect, to help your people learn new skills in preparing for presentations and actually giving them. Encourage members of the team to take turns being responsible for giving formal presentations to you and other managers (but remember that not all monitoring need be formal).

One important ground rule is to establish a regular format or schedule to provide you with information. At the very least, you should require formal reports on a monthly basis and, depending on how active your teams are in solving problems, receive informal reports more often.

Here are some options for monitoring:
- Have the team write reports.
- Hold special meetings.
- Attend meetings occasionally (all or part of the meeting) to get an update.
- Ask people to come by and see you or seek them out to provide you with an informal update.
- Have brief reports at regular department/organization meetings.

Handling Recommendations

The ultimate decision regarding whether or not to accept a team's recommendation rests with the manager of the team. This is another important ground rule that should be made clear up front, before teams begin their problem solving. It is very important that you make a decision about the recommendation(s) as quickly as possible, however, since your people will have put a great deal of work into solving a problem and need your feedback. Likewise, if you accept the recommendation(s) you will want to keep the momentum going for the implementation stage, and the longer you hold off, the more people will think you are either uncommitted to solving the problem or take little interest in their contributions.

The ultimate decision regarding implementation, however, also rests with the manager. Here again, it is important that you take timely action to get the implementation underway; take advantage of the synergy created by the problem-solving team's efforts.

There are three options with regard to the implementation of problem-solving team recommendations. These are:

1. The problem-solving team may be chartered to oversee the implementation of its recommendations.
2. Implementation may become the responsibility of the relevant manager, managers, or other groups.
3. The problem-solving team may be restructured and then chartered to implement the recommendations.

In cases where the recommended changes will affect more than one organizational unit several alternative approaches may be taken to implementation. These are:

- A task force could be formed that includes representatives of the affected units who will be responsible for implementation.
- The appropriate group of managers could oversee implementation.
- The managers of the affected units could jointly oversee implementation.
- If the pieces of implementation are fairly discrete, the individual units can independently handle the implementation of their pieces.

Just as there are advantages to forming a cross-organizational problem-solving team to study and solve a problem, there are similar benefits in putting together a cross-organizational implementation team:

- To balance or confront vested interests in the face of the need to change.
- To address conflicting approaches or views.
- To avoid precipitous action and explore a variety of effects.
- To create an opportunity and enough time to properly implement a solution.
- To develop and educate people through their participation: new skills, new information, new contacts.

Managing the Interfaces: Coordinating and Communicating Team Actions with Other Areas of the Organization

Coordination

In some cases, the problems that you will be trying to solve through teams will require coordination with other work areas or organizations. The actual coordination of the problem-solving can take two forms:

1. The problem-solving team is cross-organizational and is supervised by two or more managers representing the work areas involved.
2. The problem-solving team is composed entirely of members in your area, but the problem or its solution will have some impact on other work areas — a matter of interdependency.

In either of these cases the manager(s) involved in supervising the teams and coordinating the work must be especially attentive to the demands placed on each organization, balancing the schedules, and helping to smooth the interaction between the members of each organization involved. Most important, this requires using a collaborative management style instead of invoking direct authority (unless it is absolutely necessary to do so — as a last resort).

A manager who is supervising a problem-solving team under either condition 1 or 2 above may have responsibility for the following activities. You may be asked by members of the problem-solving team or you may decide to intervene to:

- Troubleshoot when the team runs into problems gaining cooperation from other areas when they need access to information, resources, or the support of other managers or professionals.
- Inform the manager of another organization that may be affected by a problem or its resolution (or is simply interested in how you solve it); keep these other managers notified of the progress you make, the major decisions reached, and your estimate of the impact on his or her organization (e.g., changes in scheduling, procedures, demands on staff time, etc.).
- Inform the manger of another organization when a team is working on a "common" problem, or one that will impact his or her work area, and will therefore need to get information, resources, or cooperation from that manager. Let this person know that the team has your "blessing" to work on the problem and that you are supporting it 100 percent.

Communication

As pointed out in a previous chapter on monitoring, it is most important to have frequent and high quality communication about the progress and results of quality and productivity improvement. For a number of reasons, it is valuable

154

to have a good system of information sharing so that everyone will know the results of your activities. In many cases such communication will be unnecessary because the team may be composed of the entire work area and therefore everyone will be well aware of the problem-solving team's work. But whenever this is not the case, it would be wise to put a good deal of thought into the various ways and times when others in the organization should be informed about problem-solving team activities.

Generally, the problem that a team addresses will be quite central to the work and environment of an area; therefore your subordinates will be interested in any changes which the teams are designing. Their cooperation in ultimately implementing (or not standing in the way of) the recommended changes will have a significant impact on the successful implementation of the project. One of the best ways to involve people in the changes they will be asked to support is to give them as much information as possible every step of the way about what changes are in the works. This will also counteract one of the most powerful impediments that the teams may face to final acceptance and use of their ideas: fear of the unknown.

Here are some guidelines that you can use and encourage problem-solving teams to use about when and how to communicate with others about the work and results of their team:

- Inform others at the very beginning about the problem the team is addressing.
- As appropriate, ask for input regarding the concept of the problem, its causes, and solutions.
- Inform others all along the way of the point at which the team has arrived and any progress thus far.
- Let people know when they can reasonably expect results.
- Inform others as soon as possible about the team's recommendations.
- Fully explain the likely impact of the proposed changes on people's work routines.
- Inform people as soon as possible about the final decision regarding the acceptance by management of the team's recommendations.
- Inform people regularly of the progress being made in implementation.
- Clearly communicate results of the process: fewer quality defects, improved performance, etc.

There are a variety of vehicles teams can use to communicate with others. This will depend on the type of information they wish to communicate and the 'style' your area is accustomed to. Some means of communication teams in your organization could use include:

- Periodic memoranda.
- Problem-solving team newsletter.
- Problem-solving team bulletin board.
- Brief meetings.
- Informal conversation.
- Formal presentations.

_____ Inform others at the very beginning about the problem the team is addressing.

_____ As appropriate, ask for input regarding the concept of the problem, its causes, and solutions.

_____ Inform others along the way of the point at which the team has arrived and any progress thus far.

_____ Let people know when they can reasonably expect results.

_____ Inform others as soon as possible about the team's recommendations.

_____ Fully explain the likely impact of the proposed changes on people's work routines.

_____ Inform people as soon as possible about the final decision regarding the acceptance by management of the team's recommendations.

_____ Inform people regularly of the progress being made in implementation.

_____ Clearly communicate results of the process: fewer quality defects, improved performance, etc.

Checklist: How and When Problem-Solving Teams Should Communicate Outside the Team

Providing Rewards and Recognition

Your final responsibility as a manager of the quality and productivity improvement process is to ensure that the efforts of team members are appropriately recognized. There are many different ways to recognize the contributions your subordinates make; unfortunately, we rarely take advantage of most of them. (See the checklist at the end of this section.)

Recognition is an important part of good management practice for several reasons:

- Recognition will help create an environment that motivates your people to commit themselves to your quality or productivity improvement efforts.
- Recognition is a way for your organization to express its acknowledgment of and appreciation of managers and employees who have worked hard and well to further the goals of quality and productivity improvement.
- Recognition is a way for the organization to give something *to* employees and managers.
- Recognition helps to reinforce a culture of pride and sense of being "winners."
- Recognition helps reinforce teamwork in your organization.
- Recognition bolsters self-esteem.

Everyone knows that recognition for doing a good or outstanding job is important to give to the people who work for us, but for the most part we are too caught up in whatever task is at hand to give recognition the thought and time that it deserves. The objective of this section is to learn about the ways that recognition can be an effective source of support for the process. Giving people recognition for their work can be a powerful tool to create an environment which will motivate them to feel committed to the goals and to give it their best effort.

We all know the effect that recognition can have when it has been given to us after we have worked long and hard on something. While ultimately everyone seeks recognition in the form of salary increases and job promotion (and good work in problem-solving should affect decisions about pay and position), the many other forms of recognition can have an unexpectedly powerful impact. People, when they have been recognized, feel that they are valued by other people and by the company, that their work is noticed and followed, and that they have set a visible standard of achievement which they will want to maintain. In short, recognition is a powerful way to create an environment that motivates people. Problem solving can require a tremendous amount of sustained effort and commitment in order to produce the kind of results one hopes for. As part of the job of being a manager responsible for the success of quality or productivity improvement in your area you should be prepared to utilize this tool to its maximum. Besides, it is just plain good management to recognize people when they have worked hard.

But recognition is important for another reason as well. Quality and productivity improvement asks a lot of people. Everyone is expected to work harder and better, and to change the way they work. People must change and improve so that quality or higher productivity can become the standard in your organization. Recognition is one of the ways that the organization can, in a sense, give something back to you and other managers and employees. Through recognition you can express the organization's acknowledgment and appreciation of everyone who has worked hard and well to further the goals of quality or productivity improvement.

Beyond changing the way we work, another way to bring about some changes is to influence your "corporate culture." Providing recognition can be an effective way to support these culture changes. In fact, as we all know, one of the problems with the culture of many organizations is that there is not enough recognition provided by anyone at any level.

Recognition can support the culture change in many ways:

- It can reinforce a culture of pride and a sense of being "winners." You feel and act more like a winner when someone has let you know that they perceived you as a winner. Since recognition is often public, it will foster and create an environment of many winners, which is far better than just a few or none.
- Recognition can reinforce teamwork when it is given to a team that has worked well together to solve a quality problem.
- Recognition is a way of saying, "I'm glad you are part of our team and we all recognize that you have made a contribution to our joint goals." So, it also reinforces a sense of belonging to a bigger organizationwide effort, rather than being an isolated, beleaguered, or forgotten part of the company.
- Then, of course, recognition and the satisfaction it brings will help to create a better quality of work life in your area. This occurs in part because people feel better about themselves when they know that others think highly of their work. Recognition bolsters people's self-esteem.

You can provide recognition in a variety of ways. There are two primary ways: formal and informal. The formal systems can be designed and implemented at any level of your organization from corporate on down. The informal systems are provided on a personal basis by individual managers and supervisors again at every level of the company.

Formal corporate and division-wide recognition systems are effective and an important part of recognition for problem solving, but ultimately they generally affect only a few people and their impact is limited. The informal recognition managers provide on a daily basis can be a far more powerful tool than the formal systems. After all, you and your peers will reach many more people than the formal system will and it will be on a personal and, therefore, more powerful level. The point is to avoid the common mistake of underestimating the positive impact that you as an individual manager can have on your staff's motivation and commitment. The fact is that you will have a far greater impact than the formal systems will and that most of the responsibility for providing this "fuel" for successful problem solving rests on your shoulders.

There are a number of ways that you can provide recognition for your people. Some of these you may have consciously thought through and come up with a plan for, and others you may do naturally, without necessarily thinking it through. The question is, barring giving raises and promotions, what can you do to recognize people? Here are some suggestions for ways managers can say thanks:

- When an issue arises that is similar to one an employee has shown interest in, try to involve that person in the discussion, analysis, and development of recommendations.
- Give special assignments to people who have shown initiative.
- Mention the outstanding work or idea brought to your attention by an employee at staff meetings.
- Say hello to employees when you pass by their desks or pass them in the hall.
- Have coffee or lunch with an employee or a group of employees.
- Say thanks to your boss, your peers, and employees when they have done something well or have done something to help you.
- When an employee or group presents an idea or suggestion thank them whether or not you are actually going to act on it. Thank them for their concern and initiative.
- When you are discussing an employee's or group's idea with other people, peers, or higher management make sure that you give them credit.
- Mention the latest contributions of your employees and problem-solving teams at meetings with your peers and management.
- Present "state-of-the-place" reports periodically to your employees and acknowledge the work and contributions of individuals and groups.
- Ask your boss or someone higher up to send a letter of acknowledgment or thanks to individuals or groups who have been making significant contributions.
- When possible introduce your peers and management to individuals and groups who have been making significant contributions and acknowledge their work.
- Ask your boss to attend a meeting with your employees in which you thank individuals and groups for their specific contributions.
- Ask individuals and groups to be part of or make presentations of their ideas and recommendations to higher management and to their own peers.

(You can use the checklist at the end of this section to assess your current approach to informal recognition and to plan changes in this.)

In addition to providing recognition on an informal, individual basis you can also design somewhat more structured means to recognize people and teams for their contributions to quality or productivity improvement. Here are some ideas:

- Send a letter to every team member when they establish a team thanking them for their involvement.
- Briefly attend the first meeting of a team and express your appreciation for their involvement.
- Hold a luncheon meeting with every team once they have interim findings. Express your appreciation and provide the lunch.
- Hold a thank you ceremony at the completion of a team's work. Provide breakfast, lunch, or refreshments. Invite their peers and higher management if possible.
- Send a letter to every team member at the termination of their work thanking them for their contribution.
- Establish a place to display information, posters, and pictures thanking individual employees and teams and describing their contributions.

To wrap up this exploration of recognition it is important to keep some things in mind when you think about how you will actually give informal recognition. Many managers probably have thought these issues through already, but we all tend to forget some of these things. First of all, we've seen now the many ways to provide recognition and it sometimes seems that there just isn't enough time to do everything we know we ought to do, so saying "thanks" to our people tends to slip through the cracks. But recognition really doesn't take that much time; you just have to remember to do it and to make it part of the way you manage and deal with people.

Another trap that we often fall into is to recognize only those few people who on rare occasions rise to unparalleled heights in their work. We tend to forget those who have put in extra effort on a project or who generally can be relied on to do excellent work. One of the points raised here is to try to spread the recognition around to all the people who deserve it and could use it.

Unfortunately, one of the things that your people watch about your behavior most closely and can feel the most strongly about is the way you handle recognition. So it is important to think about whether you are perceived as being fair and equitable in this regard. Otherwise, it could backfire and create unexpected hard feelings.

Lastly, some people withhold praise because they fear that standards of performance will be lowered if people find it too easy to obtain praise. As long as you continue to give negative feedback whenever it is called for, praise and recognition will not undermine your performance standards. Quite the opposite, people will feel more motivated to achieve them if they know their work and effort will be recognized and appreciated.

Actions	What I Do Now	What I Plan to Do
Greet employees when you pass by their desks or pass them in the hall.		
Have coffee or lunch with an employee or a group of employees.		
Thank your boss, peers, and employees when they have done something well or have done something to help you.		
Thank employees or groups for ideas or suggestions whether or not you are actually going to act on them. Thank them for their concern and initiative.		
Give credit where it's due when discussing an idea with other people, peers, or higher management.		
Involve employees in the discussion, analysis, and development or recommendations of issues they have shown interest in.		
Give special assignments to people who have shown initiative.		
Mention the outstanding work or idea brought to your attention by an employee at staff meetings.		
Mention the latest contributions of your employees and corrective action teams at meetings with your peers and management.		
Present "state-of-the-place" reports periodically to your employees and acknowledge the work and contributions of individuals and groups.		
Ask your boss or someone higher up to send a letter of acknowledgment or thanks to individuals or groups who have made significant contributions.		
Introduce your peers and management to individuals and groups who have made significant contributions and acknowledge their work.		
Ask your boss to attend a meeting with your employees in which you thank individuals and groups for their specific contributions.		
Ask individuals and groups to be part of or make presentations of their ideas and recommendations to higher management and to their own peers.		

Checklist: Some Ways Managers Can Say "Thanks"

Actions	What I Plan To Do
Send a letter to every problem-solving team member when they establish a team, thanking them for their involvement.	
Briefly attend the first meeting of a problem-solving team and express your appreciation of their involvement.	
Hold a luncheon meeting with every problem-solving team once they have interim findings. Express your appreciation and provide the lunch.	
Hold a thank you ceremony at the completion of a team's work. Provide breakfast, lunch, or refreshments. Invite their peers and higher management if possible.	
Send a letter to problem-solving team members at the termination of their work thanking them for their contribution.	
Establish a place to display information, posters, pictures, and so on thanking individual employees and problem-solving teams and describing their contributions.	

Checklist: Structured Ways for Management to Recognize Employees' Contributions to Productivity/Quality Improvement

Indicators of Management Commitment

When quality and productivity improvement is implemented on a widespread basis involving many organizational units, top management will need to take a strong role in supporting the initiative and making appropriate changes in policies, procedures, and systems. The efforts of middle and lower level managers on their own will not be sufficient to ensure a successful effort. It is necessary for top management to demonstrate a strong and sustaining commitment to quality and productivity to ensure that managers and employees down through the ranks take the new effort seriously and persevere in their efforts to incorporate the new practices into the regular operations and systems. But beyond merely providing a show of support, senior management should act to ensure that adequate planning and coordination activities are undertaken, that resources to support quality and productivity are available, and that the relevant changes in systems, such as communication, monitoring, and performance appraisal, are made. Without the active support and continued involvement of top management an organization-wide quality and productivity improvement effort is unlikely to succeed.

The following is a basic guide to the types of activities and roles which are the responsibility of top management in the process:

1. *Develop Plans and Set Direction*
   - Develop plans for quality and productivity
     - Strategic
     - Operational
     - Implementation
   - Hold a number of planning meetings on quality and productivity.
   - Involve a wide variety of people in the planning exercises including those who have not been involved in the past.
   - Hold routine planning meetings periodically to review plans and make mid-course corrections.

2. *Set Corporate Policy and Philosophy*
   - Develop corporate policy on quality and productivity and its implementation:
     - Policy is clear.
     - Policy is specific enough to be used and monitored.
     - Policy is in written form.
     - Policy has been communicated to everyone in many different ways.
     - Policy is understood in the same way by everyone.
     - Policy changes some old ways and legitimizes new ones.
     - Policy binds top management as well as middle management.

3. *Provide Leadership*

- Make speeches and presentations on quality and productivity goals and progress.
- Participate in regular meetings of all sorts about quality and productivity.
- Be available for discussions and meetings about quality and productivity.
- Reinforce quality and productivity in meetings on other related issues.
- Model behavior with direct staff and others in accordance with quality and productivity.
- Be involved visibly in furthering quality and productivity.

4. *Communicate*

- Establish a single communication vehicle for the entire organization to update people on quality and productivity progress and results.
- Create other channels of communication.
- Create channels for communication up the hierarchy as well as down and across.
- Open up channels of communications so that more people have access to more information.
- Send managers and employees periodic letters/memos on corrective goals, progress, and results.

5. *Delegate Authority*

- Delegate appropriate responsibilities to lower level management and task forces.
- Ensure that, in general, judgments are made at the lowest possible level in the organization.
- Ensure that top management spends less time on operational details (having delegated this) and more on providing overall direction.
- Reduce "second guessing" the decisions of subordinates.

6. *Develop Objectives and Standards*

- Develop or participate in the development of objectives, standards, and measures* for quality and productivity outcomes and results in the next six months, year, and five years.
- Develop objectives, standards, and measures for improvement in productivity and quality of services and products.
- Develop objectives, standards, and measures for the implementation of quality and productivity in the next six months, one year, and two years.
- Have regular meetings or task force to periodically review the relevancy of the objectives, standards, and measures.

---

*Measures should be designed to assist in making decisions and not for purely evaluative or performance appraisal reasons.

7. *Ongoing Management of Quality and Productivity Improvement: Monitor, Review, and Mid-Course Corrections*

- Establish a reporting system on progress and implementation.
- Hold meetings on a periodic basis to review reports.
- Track interim steps as well as final results.
- Provide adequate resources (people and dollars) to review and analyze the data.
- Provide information that is useful to and shared with all levels.

8. *Ongoing Learning: Research and Development*

- Allocate resources to research the successes and failures of quality and productivity.
- Research new ways to accomplish quality and productivity goals and fund experiments and pilot tests.
- Research the capacity of the system to produce quality services and products and to achieve higher productivity.
- Disseminate the results of the research throughout the organization.
- Provide opportunities for all levels of people to participate.

9. *Coordination*

- Hold regular meetings with direct reports to coordinate the implementation of quality and productivity.
- Ensure that all parts of the organization are moving toward the same goals with regard to quality and productivity.
- Legitimize overlap and interconnection.
- Establish vehicles for coordination, especially at lower levels in the organization.

10. *Resources*

- Allocate resources for planning.
- Allocate resources for training:
  - Top management
  - Management and supervisors
  - Quality and productivity support staff (i.e., facilitators)
  - Follow-up training
- Establish new positions for directing and supporting quality and productivity (e.g., vice president/general manager for quality and productivity)
- Allocate resources for R&D.
- Allocate resources for development, such as training tapes and materials.

11. *Personnel*

- Revise performance appraisal and reward so that people are recognized for contributions to quality and productivity.
- Develop a new career path for those responsible for implementing and supporting quality and productivity.
- Ensure that participation in this effort becomes an important step in everyone's career at the organization.

Corrective Action Steering Committees

Set priorities for departmental direction and identify quality and/or productivity problems.

Provide overall direction for quality and productivity improvement activities; set priorities, criteria, and standards; diffuse worthwhile activities.

Set the philosophy for and approve the direction of management education in quality and productivity improvement.

Solicit proposals for corrective action projects and offer funding for ideas with no other outlet.

Manage problem-solving teams (if they cross organizational lines or have organization-wide implications).

- Charter teams.
- Monitor progress.
- Approve recommendations.
- Ensure implementation.
- Provide appropriate links back to the line organization.

Serve as a forum for ensuring immediate attention to new fastbreaking issues not falling clearly within existing organizational responsibilities.

Assess periodically the "state of the organization or department" (survey data, task force results, business measures, etc.) and revise priorities, policies, and procedures accordingly for "fit" with evolving needs.

Define and provide rewards and recognition for involvement in and success with corrective action and quality and productivity improvement.

Hooking into the System: The Formation of Quality and Productivity Steering Committees

Building the Parallel Organization: Creating Mechanisms for Permanent Quality of Work Life*
(Barry A. Stein and Rosabeth Moss Kanter)

This section deals with both a need and a reality. The need: the design of organizations that are responsive to both their environments and their people, in terms of the unique character of the 1980s. The reality: Models already exist to show what a new, responsive organization might look like, and how it could be integrated with existing bureaucracies. Out of two decades or so of experience with diverse QWL activities, models have emerged that lead to what we call "parallel structures": flat, flexible, but formal problem-solving and governance organizations that serve to supplement bureaucracy and exist side by side with it, not to replace it.

The Needs of the 1980s

Bureaucracy has been long and accurately criticized for its lack of both external and internal responsiveness. Yet in the 1980s both external and internal pressures are increasing. Externally, the 1980s demands that bureaucracies respond to turbulent environments of high uncertainty, rapid change, and permeable boundaries. The oil crisis, growing inflationary pressures, market uncertainties due to foreign competition, regulatory constraints, and an antigrowth bias mean that even "mature" organizations (such as the auto industry), with mechanisms to stabilize their environments, face the need to respond more flexibly and rapidly to these environments by solving a continuing series of new problems and changing their traditional internal focus to a more external one. Internally, the 1980s demands that bureaucracies meet the rising expectations of a drastically changing labor force in a slower growth economy. These expectations will include a demand for more opportunity (career progress and the chance to develop) from a wider range of employees, including growing numbers of educated workers and women, and for more power (a sense of entitlement, more rights, and job autonomy and less "oversupervision").[1-3]

Although they affect more people and more organizations and have become more central in the 1980s, these pressures are not entirely new. We have long known that the classic Weberian bureaucracy was an oversimplified concept encompassing many different types of formal structures.[4] That conception of bureaucracy ignored the possibility that newer, more "organic" structures could be designed specifically to create flexibility and responsiveness. Such possibilities range from the matrix[5] to collectivist organizations.[6] It has been less clear whether one should talk about replacement of bureaucracy at all or if it is to be replaced, what form the replacement should take.

*The authors wish to thank Derick Brinkerhoff for his contributions to an earlier version of this section and especially Frances Grigsby for the very important role she played.

We believe that these trends of the 1980s show that the issue will be not how to *replace* bureaucracy, but how to *supplement* it. There are some tasks and conditions for which a conventional line hierarchy is better suited than any alternative. The task in the 1980s is to permit bureaucracy to function well where it can while finding a different structure capable of dealing effectively with the tasks and conditions for which bureaucracy is not suitable. The structural form emerging in the next decade that meets this criterion is what Howard Carlson at General Motors has called the "parallel organization."[7] The parallel organization is an attempt to institutionalize a set of externally and internally responsive, participatory, problem-solving structures alongside the conventional line organization that carries out routine tasks. The parallel organization is not the same as the "informal" organization that has long been recognized to coexist with a formal organization. The parallel organization is a second, equally formal structure. Nor is it an entirely *new* structure such as a matrix that replaces the previous bureaucratic structure. The parallel organization provides an additional management structure to that structure which already exists.[8]

The parallel structure thus provides a means for managing change and providing flexibility and responsiveness. These are the characteristics mentioned by Carlson[7] that account for its interest to General Motors. A second, equally important purpose, however, is served by a properly designed and managed parallel structure. It provides a source of opportunity and power above and beyond the (limited) sources in the bureaucratic structure, and this source of opportunity and power is important for people in positions least characterized by those properties. Because a sense of opportunity and power is critical to a high QWL, the parallel structure enhances individual satisfaction and effectiveness in the very act of coping with the new external pressures. The parallel structure thus forms a mechanism for building high QWL and environmental responsiveness *permanently* into bureaucratic organizations.

In this section we describe one parallel organization in detail, from the organizational needs that gave rise to it to the steps involved in developing it as a permanent structure.

Theoretical Framework

This project has as its organizing framework Kanter's structural theory of organizational behavior.[9] Key aspects of that theory are:

1. Individual effectiveness in a job is in part a function of the structural characteristics of that position — its location in the system — as well as a result of individual abilities.
2. Behaviorally, the most relevant aspects of a position within the organization are: (a) the level of opportunity, and (b) the amount of power available to the person occupying that position. Opportunity, in addition to its standard definition as "access to advancement," means challenge and the chance

to grow (increase competence and skills) and contribute to the central goals of the organization. Power means access to resources, the capacity to mobilize them, and the tools to accomplish tasks efficiently.[9-12]

3. People whose positions provide them with opportunity are highly motivated to perform; as a result they tend to develop and use their skills and knowledge productively. People who are empowered are more effective performers; they tend to support and empower their subordinates and are more strongly committed to the organization and its goals.

4. Conversely, those without opportunity withdraw; they tend to devalue their skills and lower their aspirations. Those in positions of relative powerlessness tend to become petty tyrants, resistant to change and innovation; they supervise their subordinates closely, preventing them from acquiring skills and confidence.

Based on these four principles, the project aimed at altering organizational structures. The focus was neither on job satisfaction nor the content of tasks per se, but on providing more workers with access to opportunity for career advancement and growth and access to powerful resources and relationships. Thus, the project made possible, with the guidance provided by a consulting team, a new set of organizational relationships. In contrast to some other QWL efforts, the specific work reforms were selected and carried out by the workers themselves. The parallel organization served as a primary vehicle for enabling and supporting those efforts.

Background and Setting

Compu Corp. (not its real name) is a large producer of high technology electric equipment. Although viewed from inside and out as a fast-growth company with almost unlimited potential, market conditions suggested to management in 1977 that some reorientation and evaluation of traditional practices might be in order. Three things in particular were noted:

1. Compu Corp.'s new size had made it increasingly difficult to manage traditionally.

2. Increased competition and market pressure for some products necessitated tighter control of growth and operations in those production facilities.

3. Continuing rapid developments in technology suggested a need for better anticipation of sudden product changes.

At Chestnut Ridge, one of the affected, nonunion plants, these general issues translated into more immediate concerns. Chestnut Ridge was faced with the need to control growth; moreover, there was strong pressure to reduce costs and increase productivity to maintain profit targets. Yet plant management regarded its work force, particularly the front-line production supervisors, as lacking the competence to deal effectively with these needs. Chestnut Ridge was also the lead plant for a manufacturing group — groups of trained managers and technical personnel were drawn off from time to time as the nucleus of a new facility. Yet plant management regarded many of those who would normally be promoted into vacant positions as unpromotable. Finally, new technology was already an issue at Chestnut Ridge: Some of the traditional batch manufacturing operations were being converted to assembly lines with considerable worker uneasiness resulting.

As a consequence of these pressures, the manager of personnel staff functions at Chestnut Ridge suggested to plant management the possibility of inviting Goodmeasure to propose a project that would address these issues. Funding was tentatively arranged through a central research committee, on a step-by-step basis, with each additional step to be funded contingent on the satisfactory results from preceeding steps. Compu Corp. was launching a pilot project at Chestnut Ridge with two very different objectives:

1. A developmental objective to increase the effectiveness and promotability of lower level production supervisors (and nonexempt workers who might replace them).
2. An organizational objective to increase the production organization's capacity to manage changes (e.g., assembly lines) with minimum disruption.

The resulting project, based on the framework described above, started with a hypothesis: The relatively ineffective behavior and unsuitability for promotion of many of the first-line supervisors was the result of the limited opportunity and power available to them in the existing structure. The very increased growth that had led to Compu Corp.'s success had also rendered less effective the informal processes through which both opportunity and power had been accessible. This situation was further exacerbated by the increased pressure toward control and centralization (as in the assembly line changeover). Thus, if the operating hypothesis was accurate, development and installation of a parallel organization, by providing new sources of opportunity and power, would increase participants' effectiveness and recognition. The parallel organization would also shift management's perception of employees' competence and promotability while serving as the necessary flexible structure to respond appropriately to the emerging changes.

The Project at Compu Corp.

The project at the Chestnut Ridge plant proceeded through five stages:

1. Initial education and planning.
2. Information gathering, structural diagnosis, and hypothesis testing.
3. Action planning.
4. Implementation.
5. Integration and diffusion of results within the system.

These stages were not, of course, actually sequential; there was considerable overlap. They do, however, serve to differentiate the significant elements of the project.

Stage 1

The overriding goal of the first stage was to generate understanding of and support for the project and its theoretical framework on the part of corporate and plant management and staff. The authors conducted a set of individual interviews followed by several group discussions and seminars. At these later meetings, Kanter's structural framework was presented and its relevance to organizational effectiveness at Chestnut Ridge discussed. Consultants and seminar participants then collaboratively explored the implications and what might be done.

Some (senior) people expressed doubts about the feasibility of a project which seemed to rely excessively on the as yet untested skills of those at the lower levels of the organization. Other concerns were appropriate managerial ones: Would there be an impact on compensation? Weren't the proposed activities things that the production manager should be doing? Wasn't the project challenging a company "god" — its new mechanized assembly line? As the internal organization development manager described the production manager's approval of the project: "He turned green, swallowed, clutched his heart, slid under the table, but said go ahead." Thus, doubts were dealt with openly, the rationale and hypotheses were discussed, and measurable objectives set. Despite discomfort over the possibility of failure, these exploratory sessions led to a decision to proceed.

In addition to providing forums for educational discussion (itself a structural intervention), during this stage we also created a Project Advisory Group composed of senior manufacturing and personnel managers. These managers were drawn from within and outside Chestnut Ridge in order to provide formal support and power for the activities to be undertaken. This Project Advisory Group supplied knowledgeable counsel for decisions needed for implementation, authority for plant personnel participation, sources of recognition and reward, and high-level linkages to prevent the project from floating unconnected to the rest of Chestnut Ridge and Compu Corp. Managerial participation also kept the project from appearing mysterious. From the beginning, information was made available at all levels of Compu Corp.

Stage 2

The second stage saw the systematic gathering of data, its subsequent analysis, and (eventually) its feedback to the members of the plant. To supplement what information we had already collected from informal interviews and observation, we used a formal questionnaire which provided measures of the information, flexibility, opportunities, and problems that people had in their jobs. Slightly different versions of the questionnaire were developed in collaboration with the advisory group and members of plant management and staff: one each for supervisors and direct labor (nonsupervisory personnel).

The initial hypotheses and the basic framework, as discussed with groups ranging from senior production management to direct labor, had been tentatively accepted as accurate. The formal questionnaires served two purposes: First, they refined our joint understanding of the ways our hypothesis showed up in practice and they differentiated carefully from one level to another the situation in the seven separate production groups. Second, they provided participants with more concrete and specific indication of potential roadblocks or opportunities that could profitably be addressed. The questions covered aspects of both obstacles and opportunities. (See *Sample Items from the Conditions for Work Effectiveness Survey*, page 184.)

The questionnaire was completed by 25 percent (115) of those in direct labor and 66 percent (28) of first- and second-line supervisors. Data analysis took place in several stages, but preliminary results were made available quickly to everyone who had participated in any way. Findings were presented through several short memos distributed to concerned employees through voluntary discussion sessions and through access for everyone to copies of the whole questionnaire with overall response patterns indicated. In particular, meetings were held with each production group, on a volunteer basis, to discuss the results as they affected that group. A memo was circulated to members before the meetings as was a copy of the questionnaire with group results indicated. In the memo data were presented as suggesting questions for discussion, and the meetings were conducted along similar lines. (See *Extracts from the Memo to Business Group 1*, page 183.)

The provision of written and oral feedback was also an important step in convincing people in the plant that the project represented something potentially useful. (Many employees were quite skeptical that any kind of follow-through would succeed the initial enthusiasm because in the past there had been many projects launched, but they were rarely continued.) Thus, these early activities were themselves important structures in encouraging participation in new opportunities.

Stage 3

In this stage we began to construct the elements of the parallel organization. Figure 4.1 shows its full structure in comparison with the bureaucratic line organization. Initially, a steering committee was formed which included (on an entirely volunteer basis) the plant production manager, the managers of two production groups, the plant personnel manager, a member of the employee relations staff, the personnel staff manager, and one member of the consulting team. This committee met regularly during the data collection effort and, over time, became the management of the parallel organization.

The active groups, or task forces, were created as an outcome of the data feedback meetings with the seven production groups. The action groups, as Figure 4.1 shows, were composed differently: some were existing work groups, some were mixtures of many levels, and some were groups of representatives of several areas. The action groups were offered the opportunity to continue to explore the implications of the data and to propose action plans based upon them. The structure was described (formation of task forces reporting to and represented on the steering committee) and groups were encouraged to discuss it among themselves and, if interested, with members of the steering committee itself. We, as consultants, were also available on request. The time required for this was clearly authorized as legitimate and appropriate by plant management, subject to the continuing requirement to meet agreed on business targets. Supervisors decided to use the data with their work groups in their own ways, and ultimately three "pilot" action groups enthusiastically volunteered to demonstrate the workings of the parallel organization, in consultation with the steering committee.

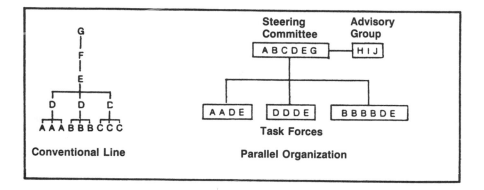

Figure 4.1 Schematic Comparison of Conventional Bureaucratic and Parallel Organization Structures

These activities were independent of, but parallel to, the internal hierarchy of the plant. As the internal personnel staff first understood the concept, the parallel structures represented the expansion of opportunity and power through:

- A chance to get training that was not strictly technical
- A chance to have impact on the company in ways other than through the immediate job.
- A way to detour around bureaucratic structures that might not be working, to see and solve their problems.
- A mechanism for managing new activities that exist outside people's jobs.

The strategy here was to create a setting for experimental action and career development that was loose enough to allow for flexibility and some trial and error, yet connected enough to the existing organization that the lessons learned could easily be seen as relevant to the larger setting and ultimately incorporated into the bureaucratic structure.

Following the guidelines of the corporate R&D committee funding the programs, and with the help of the steering committee and the consultants, on request each of the three pilot groups drew up a proposal and a plan for an action project relevant to its particular business unit. The groups presented their proposed projects directly to the R&D committee for approval. Throughout this process, and particularly in connection with the presentation to the corporate funding group, members of the pilot groups were working with, becoming known to, and recognized by people with whom they normally had no contact. Thus, access to opportunity and power was increasing steadily. Presentations of the pilot group proposals were made by teams of direct labor and first-line supervisors — people seven or eight levels lower in the hierarchy than those to whom they were presenting. All proposals were accepted enthusiastically. (They were not in competition: The ground rules were explicit.) Members of the corporate group were astonished (their statement) at what they had seen. The reappraisal of Chestnut Ridge employees had begun.

The three pilot groups elected to address different issues that were of particular significance to them and their work. In all cases the plans proposed showed understanding and acceptance of the underlying framework. The pilot groups organized themselves to make sure that they also provided more opportunity and power to participants. Pilot Group 1, which was the group most involved in the shift to an assembly line, elected to redesign the organization of the line, to reduce the disempowerment and isolation that the data indicated, and to increase productivity. The second group proposed to develop a mechanism for bringing new people on board quickly and effectively. (The data showed that people had little help in learning their jobs or their career opportunities.) The third group prepared two projects: (1) systematically attacking operational inconsistencies among the seven production groups that were responsible for many problems in production (the data showed that among the biggest headaches were intergroup transactions and flow of materials); and (2) developing, with the plant training staff, more sharply focused and timely training programs for supervisors. (The data showed that the existing programs were inadequate.) The steering committee felt that each of these projects had significant business payoffs in addition to their QWL implications.

Stage 4

In the fourth stage the pilot groups began implementing their projects. The groups' own initiative and commitment shaped the implementation process. They were free to make the key decisions about how to organize themselves, how to involve and inform direct labor, and how to maintain current production levels. Pilot group members developed specific plans and objectives, educated themselves about the topic of their particular projects (often rapidly outstripping their "expert" resources), gathered more information about Chestnut Ridge relevant to their projects, explored other resources available at Compu Corp. in general, and coordinated with each other and the steering committee as they sought to follow through with their proposals. Earlier the steering committee had added representatives from the pilot groups (representatives were chosen by their group) and met regularly to hear reports and offer guidance.

All four of the pilot group activities were completed within six months. The results were substantial. They included:

1. A strategy (subsequently implemented) to increase job effectiveness of the assembly line through the use of flexible, horizontally integrated teams and to increase productivity and product quality (measurably).
2. An employee intake and development package made up of modules that could be combined in a variety of ways to suit the needs of various users (these modules included performance appraisal training for supervisors, orientation programs for new and transferred employees regarding the production groups, and career path planning).
3. A report on procedural inconsistencies across the production groups that impeded work coordination, along with suggestions and options for action, and a recommendation for establishment of a supervisors' forum (meetings of all production supervisors). (The report was based on extensive data collected by the pilot group using a questionnaire of their own design and a series of interviews across the plant.)
4. A set of recommendations for modifying supervisory training and for making the new activities available according to perceived need on the part of supervisors themselves.

All of these results were developed by the pilot groups in collaboration with other company resources. The training and intake programs, for example, involved extensive discussions and meetings between pilot group members and people from the plant's training and personnel departments. The assembly line redesign pilot group worked closely with Compu Corp.'s manager of job design and QWL projects. This group talked to personnel in other facilities where related work was being carried out. Indeed, another assembly line group at Chestnut Ridge approached this pilot group and asked for (and got) help in setting up its own project.

Stage 5

In the fifth stage, integration and diffusion defined the central activities. The steering committee undertook presentations to others at Chestnut Ridge (including the plant manager and his staff) to inform them more fully of project activities. Project participation was incorporated into new job descriptions and made an integral part of participants' performance evaluations (linking the parallel and bureaucratic organizations). Thus, people were given job credit for work in the parallel organization. Furthermore, the products of the three pilot groups began to be applied to the problems for which they were designed.

In addition, the parallel organization embodied in the steering committee and the pilot groups was suggested as a permanent part of Chestnut Ridge. A plant charter originally written by the steering committee states that the committee represents "an opportunity for people of all levels within Chestnut Ridge to par-

177

ticipate in the experimentation of managing change. [It] also [provides] a forum in which ideas toward improving processes are developed." Thus, the parallel organization continues as a mechanism to solve problems beyond those originally identified by this particular project.

Through the occasional reports to the corporate funding committee and the meetings of the advisory group (less frequent than anyone would have liked), information about the parallel organization project continued to be available outside Chestnut Ridge. The most effective diffusion mechanism, however, was probably the link between the assembly line pilot group and Compu Corp.'s QWL manager since his function explicitly included the diffusion and exploration of any company efforts of this sort. (Establishment of such a function is, of course, in itself a structural change.)

The continuing press of Compu Corp. business and the general perception that the project at Chestnut Ridge was a special case of that factory and the production department in it, however, resulted in all of the diffusion mechanisms being less effective than any of the participants (including ourselves) would have liked. (See R. Walton's article, "The Diffusion of New Work Structures: Explaining Why Success Didn't Take," for a general discussion of the problems of diffusing work innovations.[13]) The funding committee, which had originally agreed to proceed because it seemed like a good chance "to do something for Chestnut Ridge," was pleased at what it saw, but was itself, like Compu Corp. in general, going through some important changes. All participants had a variety of other responsibilities, and this particular project seemed to be taking care of itself.

The "Other" Results

The concrete results achieved by the pilot groups were important and useful. The initial pilot groups disbanded after completing their projects. Two other, longer term results, however, deserve close attention precisely because of their potential for far-reaching effects.

The first set of results concerns project involvement for the participants themselves. Chestnut Ridge management and labor identified the following important outcomes among others: improved managerial capacity (from supervisors and direct labor), increased planning skills, broadened concern for one's own job and for Chestnut Ridge and Compu Corp. as a whole, increased motivation on the job, decreased strength of stereotypic views by both labor and management personnel, and improved use of plant resources.

In short, people in the factory who particpated in the project gained important new skills, became more productive, and in the process were more satisfied with their jobs. As one participant said, "My own personal involvement with this project has helped me a lot in developing skills I need as a supervisor. . . . I wish more people could be given the opportunity to work on the same type of project." Another (higher level) supervisor who participated as a member of one of the pilot groups was asked later how he and others had benefited from it. His reply included the following points:

- All of the people are communicating better, even over and above the project.
- I learned a little planning and gained some exposure.
- Others have seen more problems and more [styles of] supervisors — they have a larger perspective.
- We have learned how to collect and analyze data, and are learning how to diagnose from it.

"And," he added, "people who have left my staff are still continuing on the project." (Participants were not atypical; statistical tests on background data for participants and nonparticipants showed no significant differences.)

These outcomes did not go unnoticed by senior managers. Indeed, one of the key functions performed by the steering committee was to help assure the integration of project-related activities and results into formal performance appraisal, salary review, and promotion/selection processes. (This was only possible because the membership of the steering committee included some senior managers with appropriate authority.) The efforts of the steering committee led to some explicit actions that were entirely traceable to the project and that bore directly on one of the initial objectives — i.e., solving the problem of a lack of promotable people.

- Several participants received 5 to 15 percent raises based on their project performance; they would otherwise have received no raise.
- Several people in both direct labor and supervisory categories were reappraised as more promotable than had previously been assumed. One supervisor, who had been ranked in the middle of all the production supervisors, was moved to the top of the list.
- Several people who had been considered unpromotable were in fact promoted. At least one of these involved a transfer into an entirely different function than would normally have been considered.

The second set of results concerns the creation of a parallel operating structure and a demonstration that the structure could function side by side with the existing bureaucratic factory structure while providing an alternative vehicle for generating and distributing opportunity and power. The results just outlined provided company decision makers with enough evidence of the merit and potential of the parallel organization to consider institutionalizing and extending it as a formal structure in the plant.

The Significance of Parallel Organization Structures

The concept of a parallel organization has been used occasionally by those engaged in promoting QWL. But we think it has not been systematically applied with a full understanding of its significance for either QWL practice or organization theory. Most of the specific elements of our project were not unique in and of themselves; most would be endorsed by a variety of organizational theorists and change schools. The unique contribution and significance of the project reported here is the conceptual framework surrounding it. We believe this framework exhibits the characteristics necessary for successful work reform in the 1980s.

The opportunity-power framework shows the importance of the ways people are connected to an organization — namely, their location in career and resource-distribution structures. The parallel organization provides a vehicle for creating new ways of flexibly grouping people, providing the possibility of challenge, learning, and growth (opportunity), and for opening access to resources, support, and recognition (power). It cuts across the bureaucratic hierarchy and existing functional distinctions. The creation of a parallel organization structure constitutes the central reform and the major change rather than the immediate results generated by elements of the parallel organization from time to time. There has typically been some confusion here. Specific changes (e.g., team assembly methods, new communication vehicles, or more open career access) are often equated with "work reform" itself. For example, the Volvo QWL experience has often been described in terms of a new technology and team assembly. We regard those as just two specific manifestations of an extensive set of structural changes that involved decentralization and creation of parallel problem-solving and decision-making vehicles. We suggest instead that the establishment of a modified structure is the more critical point.[14, 15]

The parallel organization concept also suggests some revisions in organization theory. Our experience shows that it is possible for a mechanistic and an organic organization to exist side by side, carrying out different but complementary tasks. These two kinds of organizations are not necessarily opposites. They are different mechanisms for involving people in organizational tasks.

The mechanistic organization is the maintenance-oriented, operating hierarchy: It defines job titles, pay grades, a set of relatively fixed reporting relationships, and related formal tasks. In the mechanistic organization opportunity tends to be limited to formal promotion paths, and power flows from the contacts and resources inherent in a defined position. The main function of the mechanistic organization is the maintenance of production and the system that supports it — that is, the continuing routinization of useful procedures.

The organic organization, on the other hand, is change-oriented and embodied in the parallel structure. People are grouped temporarily in a number of different ways as appropriate to the problem-solving tasks at hand. They are not limited by their position in the hierarchy. A different set of decision-making channels and "reporting relationships" operates, and the organization as a whole is more flexible and flat. In this more fluid, parallel structure, opportunity and power can be expanded far beyond what is available in the bureaucratic organization. The main task of the parallel organization is the continued reexamination of routines; exploration of new options; and development of new tools, procedures, and approaches. It seeks to institutionalize change. As their utility is demonstrated, the *new* routines can be transferred into the bureaucratic organization for maintenance and integration. The differences in the two kinds of organizations are indicated in Table 4.1.

Bureaucratic Organization

- Routine operations — low uncertainty
- Focused primarily on "production"
- Limited "opportunities" (e.g., promotion)

- Fixed job assignments
- Competency established before assignment
- Long chain of command
- Objectives usually top-down
- Rewards: pay/benefits

- Functionally specialized
- Leadership is a function of level

Parallel Organization

- Problem solving — high uncertainty
- Focused primarily on "organization"
- Expandable "opportunities" (e.g., participation in a task force)
- Flexible, rotational assignments
- Developmental assignments

- Short chain of command
- Objectives also bottom-up
- Rewards: learning, recognition/visibility, different contribution, bonus possibility, new contacts
- Diagonal slices — mix functions
- Leadership drawn from any level

Table 4.1 Characteristics of Bureaucratic and Parallel Organizations

The simultaneous availability and operation of parallel and bureaucratic structures provide a basis for the efficient operation of each because both are equally formal structures, able to carry out their specialized functions directly. This idea is not encompassed by any of the current approaches to thinking about organizational structure. It calls attention to people's potential for simultaneous involvement in a work organization in two different ways and through two different, equally formal structures.

Such a structure is quite different from several other alternatives aimed at some of the same objectives. The parallel organization is not a matrix which primarily deals with reporting relationships and expands the mechanistic structures without modifying their intrinsic properties. It is precisely the mechanistic properties that render matrixes difficult to apply in practice. The parallel organization does share the notion of multiple vehicles of authority and accountability with the matrix. It is not a variant of project organization since it involves a formal structure for continual self-extension and self-modification. Finally, the parallel organization is not an informal organization since it is official, acknowledged, possessed of its own independent management structure, and linked to the rest of the organization.

181

Conclusion

Organizations in the 1980s will be faced with two continuing problems to which the notion of a parallel organization is particularly applicable. First, increasingly turbulent environments will be the rule. Organizations will need to be more aware of these currents and able to respond to them rapidly and appropriately. This turbulence will include both market and nonmarket pressures. Effective response is not a task to which bureaucracy is well suited.[16] Second, trends in the labor force and the economy will result in a growing opportunity squeeze, with more people wanting jobs of the kind that will be in ever-shorter supply because of reduced growth. The notion of a permanent parallel organization directly addresses these issues by: (1) greatly expanding the job opportunities other than promotion that are available to people; and (2) institutionalizing and developing methods based on temporary jobs and tasks.

We suggest that the parallel organization may be a significant answer to the problem of how to reform industrial and other organizational work in general. The workers (including managers and professionals) do it themselves through their participation in the parallel organization. Managers can support it because it does not undercut their own positions, nor replace their functions. On the contrary, managers, as well as workers, can benefit by taking advantage of these new developments and the opportunities they represent. The lessons of the parallel organization are brought back to the bureaucratic organization *without replacing it. Both* function side by side. The issue is not how to change conventional hierarchical bureaucracies; that problem has proven to be so recalcitrant as to appear nearly impossible to some.[17] Rather through the creation of parallel structures, *alternatives* bureaucracy can be fashioned alongside it.

This is the key point. A second, formal structure oriented to QWL and flexibility can be erected not on the ruins of bureaucracy, but on its living capacity to do what bureaucracy does best.

One way we've been using the information that you provided us through the questionnaires is to take a closer look at each of the business groups and the differences among them. Following are some highlights about group 1 and some of the questions that they suggest:

Supervisors

- The more flexibility you have in your job, the fewer headaches to take care of. Flexibility seems helpful. What kinds of flexibility particularly help in this connection? In what ways? If this is true, how can jobs be made more flexible?

- You generally feel that there are many different jobs available for you to advance to, but you don't seem completely sure what they are. What might be done to help you to get more of this information?

Direct Labor

- The more time spent at Compu Corp., the greater the number of things that might hurt your chances for promotion, raises, advancement, etc. Why is this? Does this mean that the more time in the organization, the more these things become known or is there a real change?

- Training and learning around your jobs are very important — some of you said you don't have skills, training, and knowledge that you need or at least as much of it as you would like. Some of you said that you have skills, training, and knowledge that don't get used in your jobs. How can this be changed?

- Many of you are somewhat dissatisfied with your opportunities for advancement. They seem more limited, less clear than you would like. Is there something that might be done about this?

Extracts from the Memo to Business Group 1

Opportunities

1) How much do you *have* now?

2) How much would you *like to have* now?

	None at all	A fair amount		A lot		Much less than I have now	As much as I have now		Much more than I have now

The chance to gain new skills and knowledge on the job.

1 2 3 4 5   1 2 3 4 5

The chance to learn about how the company works.

1 2 3 4 5   1 2 3 4 5

Headaches

1) How *often* do they occur?

2) How *easy* are they to take care of?

| | Never | | Sometimes | | Very often | Very easy | | Neither easy nor difficult | | Very difficult |

Reorganizing to produce a new product or provide a new service.

1 2 3 4 5   1 2 3 4 5

Dealing with people in other departments

1 2 3 4 5   1 2 3 4 5

Flexibility in Decision Making

1) How much flexibility *do you have?*

2) How much flexibility *do you need?*

| | Out of my hands | | Consulted | | Act on my own | Much less than I have now | | As much as I have now | | Much more than I have now |

Contacting the people you need to be in touch with.

1 2 3 4 5   1 2 3 4 5

Deciding how the work in your unit gets done.

1 2 3 4 5   1 2 3 4 5

Information

1) How much knowledge do you have?

2) How much knowledge do you need?

| | No knowledge | | Some knowledge | | Know almost everything | Much more than I have now | | As much as I have now | | Much less than I have now |

The relationship of the work in your unit to the work of the company.

1 2 3 4 5   1 2 3 4 5

What more senior managers think about the work of your unit.

1 2 3 4 5   1 2 3 4 5

Sample Items from the Conditions for Work Effectiveness Survey

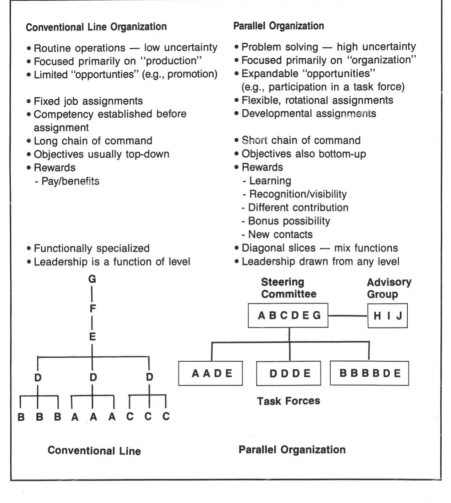

Conventional Line Organization

- Routine operations — low uncertainty
- Focused primarily on "production"
- Limited "opportunties" (e.g., promotion)
- Fixed job assignments
- Competency established before assignment
- Long chain of command
- Objectives usually top-down
- Rewards
  - Pay/benefits
- Functionally specialized
- Leadership is a function of level

Parallel Organization

- Problem solving — high uncertainty
- Focused primarily on "organization"
- Expandable "opportunities" (e.g., participation in a task force)
- Flexible, rotational assignments
- Developmental assignments
- Short chain of command
- Objectives also bottom-up
- Rewards
  - Learning
  - Recognition/visibility
  - Different contribution
  - Bonus possibility
  - New contacts
- Diagonal slices — mix functions
- Leadership drawn from any level

Characteristics of Conventional Line and Parallel Organizations

(Source: Barry Stein and Rosabeth Moss Kanter. "Building the Parallel Organization: Toward Mechanisms for Permanent Quality of Work Life." *Journal of Applied Behavioral Science*, 16 (1980): 371-388.)

Creating a Supportive Organizational Environment

Critical Success Factors

The objectives of this section are listed as follows:

- To identify the various components of the factors in the work environment that are critical to the success of the Corrective Action Process.
- To define the action steps that will support each critical success factor.
- To consider your own and your people's requirements for the work environment.
- To develop an action plan for establishing critical success factors or reinforce existing ones.

A point that cannot be emphasized enough is that quality and productivity improvement are not magical processes that are guided by the hidden or invisible hand. Neither are they a simple result of adding sophisticated technology to remove "human error." First and last, quality and productivity gains occur through people and the way in which people are managed. This includes both the formal and informal practices of management, the unofficial rules and norms as well as the values of management. All of these together comprise the culture of an organization and the way in which people are treated.

The successful implementation of the Quality/Productivity Improvement Process is directly tied to the culture of the work area. By putting into use the concepts and ideas you have learned you will be working to change the culture of your work area. At the same time, the critical success factors — those written and unwritten rules — will help determine how successful you are in implementing the corrective action process.

The critical success factors include several key areas of the work environment, and in some ways are the foundation of an organization. They include:

- The factors that encourage good communication which is necessary to make the process work; this means both the formal communication process through meetings, memos, and other paperwork, as well as the informal processes — do people talk with one another, with you, and with those in other parts of the organization?
- Creating an environment that encourages people to set quality or productivity improvement goals; people should see value in improving the level of quality or productivity in their area, for both themselves and the organization. They should be willing to set goals to do this.
- Creating an environment in which people will maintain the highest standards of performance; people should be motivated to give their best at work and to know that they will be recognized and appreciated by the organization for doing so.

- Giving people the self-esteem and tools to take initiative to solve problems; people should be "empowered" to take action; they will be reluctant to get involved if they feel they lack the tools — the expertise and knowledge, resources, and management support — as well as the inner confidence to take on and resolve quality or productivity problems.

Sometimes it is possible to learn a lot about how to do something right by first examining how to do it completely wrong. *Rules for Stifling Innovation* (page 191) following this section present some "anti-success" factors. In some companies these rules are actively practiced as if they were an official credo and posted on the walls of the building. One can easily imagine how a Corrective Action Process would work in an organization where managers operated with this set of rules.

The critical success factors that provide a positive enviroment where quality is encouraged involve just the opposite of these rules for stifling innovation. These factors follow this section.

There are many specific ways that managers and supervisors can build these critical success factors into their work. If you incorporate these suggestions into your own management style you will not only increase the chances of making the Corrective Action Process work, but you will help to change the culture in your organization in a very positive way.

Receptiveness to new ideas:
- Invite "action proposals" from employees on concrete ideas — these are more useful than vague suggestions.
- Try to listen to new ideas first without evaluating or passing judgment.
- When people give you an idea that is promising, but needs improvement, encourage them to think more about it, don't write off the idea.

Provide easy access to information:
- Share information about the rest of the organization soon after you receive it — this speeds up the information flow.
- Establish mechanisms to disseminate information on a regular basis.
- Learn from your people about their information needs, both the content (what kind of information) and how often they need certain types of information.
- Hold regular office hours when your people can count on you to be around to answer questions.
- Get one of your people to accompany you to meetings so they can get access to information first hand and receive some visibility to other managers.

Give rapid approval with a minimal amount of red tape:
- Establish early deadlines for responding and hold yourself to these. Let your employees know what your deadlines are.

- Try to give early "blessings" when people seek your approval on a project. Give them a "go ahead" on the development of the project as soon as you can.
- Avoid seeking "shotgun" approval from peers or managers higher up which may require more time. Get approval for your own or subordinates' projects from only the most essential sources.
- Make a decision early on about which managers need to approve a project and which managers may only need to be informed about what you are doing. Since approvals generally take longer you will save time by shortening your list of people who need to approve versus those who only need to know.
- When your subordinates make requests for resources back them up and negotiate for them with other managers or organizations; this will speed up the project by getting your people the materials and other resources they need as soon as possible.

Provide abundant praise and recognition. This not only helps to motivate people, but shows them that their efforts were noticed and valued by others in the organization.

- Send out letters of thanks for good jobs — a relatively easy task for you — by sending a copy to your manager and the personnel file. People will be grateful for the visibility you provided them.
- "Talk up" your good people outside the work area, especially to higher managers. Again, your employees will respond well to the visibility this provides them and it gives you "good press" when others know about the performance of your work area.
- You will also get a positive response from your people if you create new rewards for good performance, both formally and informally (lunches, dinners, "attaboys," etc.). People like to be appreciated, even in small ways. What is important is that you notice the contributions of your people since this helps to build their self-esteem and a culture of "pride" in the organization.

Provide clarity about career opportunities. Help people to think and plan about their future and development in your organization.

- Hold meetings with individuals about their goals and skills. Let them know you're interested in their plans and helping to achieve them.
- Get information to people about career paths and how to prepare for them. People may become committed to their present task if they know it leads to something even more challenging in the future.
- Create "development plans" for and with each person in your area. Not only will people feel more committed to your organization since they can envision a future for themselves, but they will appreciate your concern for their career.

- Inform people about openings when you hear of them. This will give them a chance to pursue their career plans and share their skills with the rest of the organization.

Provide clarity about performance standards. Your people will know all of your expectations for their work and have some way to measure their own performance. It will also help you create some "yard sticks" to judge their efforts fairly and whether or not people are truly meeting your expectations.

- Hold regular performance reviews and evaluations. This keeps people up-to-date on your standards and how well they measure up.
- Give frequent feedback about performance, both good and bad. Many studies have shown that people are more motivated when given feedback about the work they do, and the sooner the better.
- Reward people for meeting standards. Be explicit about this — let them know what the rewards are based on. This will ensure a fair evaluation and reward process.
- Have meetings to discuss expectations for the entire work area; communicate in group meetings what you expect people to do and when. Make the behavior standards clear before the entire group, and not just to a few individuals, in the hopes that the news will trickle down.

When changes are imminent, give advance warnings and provide people with the opportunity to become involved in the change:

- Prepare people for changes by sharing information as soon as you get it. People will be more likely to trust you and feel that you are being honest with them.
- Follow the "no surprises" rule — communicate both the good and bad news, but not in ways that put people on the spot, make them embarrassed, or provoke a hostile response. Warn specific individuals ahead of time if it is more appropriate.
- Ask your people to help plan for changes. Do this by creating task forces or committees. You may find that your employees have a lot of good ideas to contribute and can remove the onus for planning all of the change from you.
- Solicit opinions from everyone in your work area about impending changes. Even if people cannot do much to avert an impending change, they will feel better if given the chance to comment on it. This may also prove a valuable source of organizational data for you — information you may need to pass on to higher management about the "readiness for change."
- Encourage cooperation and support between departments whenever possible. Sometimes this may be more formal, through problem-solving teams,

but informal collaboration may help you discover new sources of information and support for other parts of your work.

- Create teams that work across functions when this is appropriate in the Corrective Action Process, or informally if it will help get the work done more effectively. By rewarding teams and individuals for their participation it also encourages this as a positive and legitimate behavior.
- Lend subordinates to other areas when they need assistance. You may be able to "trade" some of your people on a temporary basis and get the assistance of someone with different skills from another area.
- Encourage job rotation between areas, perhaps through short internships or formal trades. This provides your people with important knowledge of how work is carried out in other areas, develops their own skills, and creates a backup supply of expertise for those times when there might be a shortage.
- Share the "glory tasks" when working with other areas. This creates good relationships and encourages cross-functional team behavior for the future. It will also help you develop good sources of support or "cheerleaders" outside your organization.
- Pass on information to other areas that may be helpful to them, especially if changes in your work will have an impact on their department. This will ensure quality across divisions and limit the possiblility of defective work.

Finally, try to practice delegation to the lowest possible level. This will not only save you time but helps to "empower" your subordinates in several ways:

- Decide which tasks can be handled at lower levels without your direct supervision. If you do this ahead of time it will make clear your expectations and also save time in determining who is eligible to complete the task.
- Give each person his or her own territory in which he or she has full responsibility. This will provide your people with a greater sense of autonomy and ownership of the tasks you stake out for them.
- Let your people schedule their own work pace individually to whatever degree this is possible. People will feel a greater sense of control over their own work when they can exercise some discretion. This is a good way to empower them.
- Let subordinates develop the means to carry assignments out. If you can provide broad assignments or output goals, let your people design the path to get there. This will almost always encourage more innovation and initiative on their part.

A summary of the ways managers can build critical success factors into their area and a worksheet to plan for actions to implement new critical success factors in your area follow this section.

1. Regard any new idea from below with suspicion because it is new and because it is from below.

2. Guard data carefully. Make people justify their requests for information; you wouldn't want data to fall into the wrong hands.

3. Insist that people who need your approval to act go through several other levels of management to get their signatures first.

4. Express your criticisms freely and withhold your praise. (This keeps people on their toes.)

5. Keep people guessing about their futures. Keep standards vague so that people never feel they've done enough.

6. Make decisions to reorganize or to change policies in secret, and spring them on people unexpectedly. (That also keeps people on their toes.)

7. Set up competitions between departments. Get them to criticize each other's proposals, and then choose the winner.

8. Never forget that you already know everything important about this business.

Rules for Stifling Innovation

(Source: Rosabeth Moss Kanter. *The Change Masters: Innovation for Productivity in the American Corporation.* New York: Simon & Schuster, 1983.)

1. Receptiveness to new ideas.

2. Easy access to information.

3. Rapid approval with minimal red tape.

4. Abundant praise and recognition.

5. Clarity about career opportunities and performance standards.

6. Advance warning of changes and a chance to be involved.

7. Cooperation and support between departments.

8. Delegation to the lowest level possible.

Critical Success Factors
(Copyright © 1983 Goodmeasure, Inc. Cambridge, MA. All rights reserved.)

Go over the list to see which of the items "fit" your actual work situation, given the kind of people you have and the kind of work they do. Check the box labelled "applies to my situation" for every item that fits at all.

Then, think about each of the "applies" items to choose the five or six items that represent your highest priorities for action: the places where you could act tomorrow with high immediate payoff for your people. Check "priority for action" for those items.

Applies to my situation	Priority for action	
		Receptiveness to New Ideas
☐	☐	• Invite "action proposals" and concrete ideas from employees, not vague suggestions
☐	☐	• Listen to new ideas first without evaluating or passing judgment
☐	☐	• Give promising ideas a second chance — ask for modification or revision, not rejection
		Easy Access to Information
☐	☐	• Share information soon after it is received
☐	☐	• Establish regular mechanisms to disseminate information — memos, meetings, conferences, etc.
☐	☐	• Learn about people's information needs
☐	☐	• Hold regular office hours to answer questions
☐	☐	• Take one person along to meetings (on a rotating basis)
		Rapid Approval with Minimal Red Tape
☐	☐	• Try to establish early deadlines for responding — inform employees of this
☐	☐	• Give early "blessings" for initial approval of projects/ideas
☐	☐	• Avoid "shotgun" approval — seek approval from only most essential sources
☐	☐	• Decide early who needs to give their approval and who needs only to be informed
☐	☐	• Back up people's request for resources — negotiate for them
		Abundant Praise and Recognition
☐	☐	• Send letters of thanks for good jobs — send copies to my manager and personnel file
☐	☐	• "Talk up" good people outside of the department
☐	☐	• Create new rewards for good performance — prizes
☐	☐	• Have special celebrations for recognition — for individuals and entire work area
		Clarity About Career Opportunities
☐	☐	• Hold meetings with individuals about their goals and skills
☐	☐	• Get information to people about career paths and how to prepare for them

Worksheet to Plan the Implementation of Critical Success Factors

Applies to my situation	Priority for action	
☐	☐	• Create "development plans" for and with each of my people — prepare them for the next step in their career
☐	☐	• Inform people of openings when you hear of them
		Clarity About Performance Standards
☐	☐	• Hold regular performance reviews and evaluations
☐	☐	• Give frequent feedback about performance — good and bad
☐	☐	• Reward people for meeting standards — let them know this
☐	☐	• Have meetings to discuss expectations for entire work area
		Advance Warnings of Changes and a Chance to be Involved
☐	☐	• Prepare people for changes by sharing information as you get it
☐	☐	• "No surprises" — communicate bad news and good news
☐	☐	• Ask your people to help plan for changes — create task force or committee
☐	☐	• Solicit opinions from everyone in the work area about impending changes
		Cooperation and Support Between Departments and Organizations
☐	☐	• Create teams that work across functions — reward and recognize for participation
☐	☐	• Lend subordinates to other areas when they require assistance
☐	☐	• Encourage job rotation between areas — short "internships" or trades
☐	☐	• When working with other areas share the "glory tasks" and the credit
☐	☐	• Pass information to other areas that will be helpful to them
		Delegation to the Lowest Level Possible
☐	☐	• Decide which tasks can be handled at lower levels without direct supervision
☐	☐	• Give each person his or her own territory in which they have full responsibility
☐	☐	• Let people schedule their own work pace individually — when to work harder, when to slow down
☐	☐	• When giving subordinates assignments let them develop the means to carry them out

Worksheet to Plan the Implementation of Critical Success Factors (cont.)

Characteristics of Effectively Managed Organizations

In the preceding section we examined the individual critical organizational factors that can promote an effective campaign to solve quality and productivity problems. However, it would be interesting and valuable to pull these elements together and develop a portrait of an organization which was run along the lines described. Just what would such an organization look like? What follows is a description of an ideal organization — one that is effectively managed and able to anticipate and solve quality and productivity problems. A useful exercise would be to compare your organization with the one described here to evaluate how close it comes to the ideal and to identify areas in which changes might be made.

1. Growth limited or controlled. Explicit decisions about how much growth can be handled, rejecting opportunities that would push the organization beyond the capacity to handle new activity or people.
2. Decentralization and divisionalization. Keeping capacity for action (e.g., needed resources) at local levels, to the extent possible. Setting size limits and creating new divisions with a complete array of functions whenever size limits are exceeded.
3. Organizational "cloning." Experienced personnel from one unit or facility form the nucleus for spinning off another new but identical unit (e.g., some plants known as training grounds or "mother plants").
4. Heavy use of internal staff personnel and consultants, on a decentralized basis, as problem solvers and integrators.
5. Explicit organizational philosophy and culture, clearly and frequently communicated, stressing "mission" and uniqueness.
6. Excellent, welfare-oriented benefits. (Sometimes more emphasis on benefits and on future growth in pay than on immediate pay.)
7. Selection systems emphasizing social as well as technical skills. (To seek people who can flourish in a relationship-oriented environment.) Selection for homogeneity of traits. Recruiting from competitors. Hiring relatively young employees without too much socialization into other kinds of organizational patterns, who cost less now and can grow later.
8. More complex formal structures. People connected for fast communication (e.g., liaisons between departments).
9. Frequent mobility across units: (a) immediate — travel facilitated by company transportation systems; (b) long-term — frequent transfers of personnel. (People rather than structures serve as carriers and transmitters of lessons from experience and help integrate the organization at lower levels, rather than only higher level managers serving as integrators.)
10. Contracting out for special services or for special projects that can be done in a fashion insulated from the rest of the organization.

11. For individuals to succeed: heavy investment in interpersonal relationships, especially information seeking.

When growth slows, then more formalization, standardization, and centralization can (and usually does) occur. For example:

Number 1: Attention can be devoted to adding efficiencies by recentralizing some common functions across divisions, or adding to their power in a matrix.

Number 4: Staff can become more centralized at a corporate level, with more central policy and explicit coordination.

Number 9: Fewer meetings, less travel, and less frequent transfers are necessary, as there is more standardization and routine, more experienced personnel, and better vertical information systems (around planning and control systems).

Number 10: Services contracted out or handled on a special project basis can be built into ongoing internal functions.

How Participative Management Can Become a Way of Life

The following are some indicators that participative management has begun to take hold:

- First, something has to *work*. So, the new practices produce results and a success experience for the people using them.
- Then the new practices are defined and known to people. People can feel their presence, attribute results to the new practices, and evaluate their use.
- People learn how to use new practices. There is training for the new skills required, and help provided for people to make the transition.
- The rewards change to support the new practices.
- The leader wants them and continues to push for them even when it looks like things might slide back.
- The new practices clearly get something for individuals: more of something they have always wished they could do.
- Structures/patterns change to support the new practices: the flow of information, the division of responsibilities, the kinds of groupings that exist, etc.
- The new practices move from being confined to a few "experimental" areas off to the side to being broadly relevant to tasks of all sorts.
- There is *momentum* and critical mass: More and more people use the new practices, they are repeated frequently and on multiple occasions. It becomes embarrassing or out-of-sync not to use them.
- They become contractual: a written or implied condition of work in this unit.
- They become a basis for the selection of people for work in this unit: Can they use the new practices?

- There is a mechanism for educating new people who enter the department in the practices — which are, by this time, no longer new but rather simply "the way we do things around here."

Organizational conditions, as well as the actions of individual managers and employees, can and do have significant impact on the ability of an organization to solve quality and productivity problems. Throughout this book we have been suggesting that in addition to the Corrective Action Process the goals of improving quality and productivity can be achieved as a result of a participative-collaborative style of management. While there are many ways that individual managers can become more participative through their own initiative, a great deal of managerial behavior is constrained and influenced by the organizational environment — structure, systems, policies, and procedures. Thus, it may be necessary to examine and change these conditions so that they encourage and enable managers to behave in a more participative fashion. Clearly, such a project would require agreement and action at a high level of management and would constitute a major change effort in and of itself. While such an undertaking may be beyond the authority of many of the readers to initiate, nevertheless it is important for all to be aware of the organizational conditions which support a participative-collaborative style of management.

- There are multiple reporting relationships, rather than a single all-powerful boss so that managers have an option if they hit a dead end in one direction, and so that they learn how to take into account and satisfy more than one perspective on a project.
- Subordinates are professionals or treated as professionals with control over their work, and options for the use of their time so that they have to be convinced to give effort and to feel included in something they can "own."
- Slack resources and many people control budgets so that they can be tapped with money and support, and they feel included and involved.
- A number of people outside the immediate work area have interest in and a stake in issues of broader concern so that few projects can be launched without including and involving others, without seeking and receiving their support.
- Top management listens to coalitions more often than to individuals and likes to know that there is widespread support across key areas for an idea or a project before endorsing it. But once the grass roots support is clear, management is also likely to reward this coalition-building by backing a project, so that an incentive is created for team and coalition-building efforts.
- Information is widely shared in many directions. The informal communication networks are very active, and managers receive a great deal of information and there is an incentive for them to provide a great deal of information because little goes on behind closed doors.

- There are broad and occasionally ambiguous assignments with the means largely unspecified.
- A free and somewhat random flow of information is encouraged, so that new opportunities are suggested to managers from unexpected places.
- Multiple connections exist among managers, e.g., several reporting relationships, cross-departmental committees, etc.
- An *ante hoc* more than *post hoc* financial and job allocation system exists in which managers get budgets (or assignments) *before* accomplishments, to use in carrying them out, rather than getting money or promotions only *after* they are completed — i.e., an investment-oriented, hope-for-future performance system instead of an award-oriented, pay-for-past performance system.
- Top management expresses willingness to invest in new initiatives.
- There are multiple centers of power with budgetary excesses that can be bid for by managers with compelling proposals.
- A high proportion of managers in line departments are staff-like, so that they must argue for a budget or find a constituency to please.
- Management makes lavish use of recognition as a reward, including publicity, contact with power holders, and reputation enhancement.
- Job security is a reality, thereby reducing the threat implied by major changes and facilitating the mobilization of subordinates.
- Long-term close working relationships exist among managers, facilitating the exchange of favors.
- The organization design encourages lateral relationships as a source of resources, information, and support, rather than vertical relationships, so that there is a tradition of working through teams and coalitions of peers.
- Bosses of middle managers operate in a supportive but hands-off fashion, providing an initial blessing and availability for visible support if needed, but otherwise stay away.
- There is easy access of managers to more senior executives other than their boss and to managers in other functions.
- Managers actively encourage diversity of approach *along with* a clear company image and pride in that image.
- Resources (financial and human expertise) are located near the people who can use them.
- Managers are frequently moved into new positions (even laterally) within a framework of long company service. This encourages a fresh start, the need to win subordinates' loyalty, competition to beat one's predecessor, the desire to make one's mark in order to get an even better next assignment, etc.
- Organizational stability derives from a coherent culture and a consistent overall set of processes and methods.

Leadership

____ Is someone clearly in charge of the project?

____ Does that person genuinely believe in the project and want to see it succeed?

____ Does that person have the skills necessary to pull off the project?

    ____ Political savvy

    ____ Connections to important people

    ____ Salesmanship

    ____ Inspires trust

    ____ Communicates readily/well

    ____ Patience

    ____ Can maintain clear view of goals, even during chaotic process

    ____ Nevertheless is flexible

    ____ Follows up

    ____ High energy

    ____ Demonstrates genuine respect for people at all organizational levels

    ____ Willing to delegate

    ____ Willing to share the glory

    ____ Listens well

Has leadership in the project been legitimized with

    ____ the leader's boss?

    ____ top management?

    ____ peers?

    ____ project participants?

____ If there is a task force, has a leader been identified and legitimized?

____ Is leadership accessible to being influenced?

____ Are there opportunities for lower level participants to take leadership responsibilities when they are ready?

Organizational Linkages

____ Is top management aware of the project?

____ Is top management on board and supportive?

____ Is there a formal steering committee or informal advisory committee of key top level people?

____ Are there clear procedures for obtaining their opinions and keeping them informed?

Checklist for Managing Corrective Action Projects

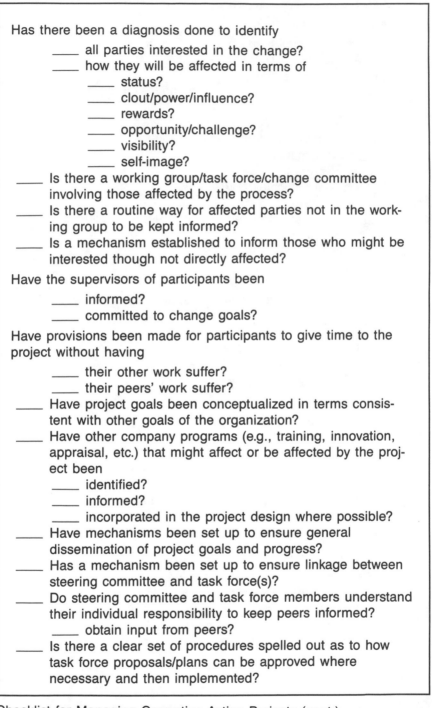

Has there been a diagnosis done to identify

_____ all parties interested in the change?

_____ how they will be affected in terms of

_____ status?

_____ clout/power/influence?

_____ rewards?

_____ opportunity/challenge?

_____ visibility?

_____ self-image?

_____ Is there a working group/task force/change committee involving those affected by the process?

_____ Is there a routine way for affected parties not in the working group to be kept informed?

_____ Is a mechanism established to inform those who might be interested though not directly affected?

Have the supervisors of participants been

_____ informed?

_____ committed to change goals?

Have provisions been made for participants to give time to the project without having

_____ their other work suffer?

_____ their peers' work suffer?

_____ Have project goals been conceptualized in terms consistent with other goals of the organization?

_____ Have other company programs (e.g., training, innovation, appraisal, etc.) that might affect or be affected by the project been

_____ identified?

_____ informed?

_____ incorporated in the project design where possible?

_____ Have mechanisms been set up to ensure general dissemination of project goals and progress?

_____ Has a mechanism been set up to ensure linkage between steering committee and task force(s)?

_____ Do steering committee and task force members understand their individual responsibility to keep peers informed?

_____ obtain input from peers?

_____ Is there a clear set of procedures spelled out as to how task force proposals/plans can be approved where necessary and then implemented?

Checklist for Managing Corrective Action Projects (cont.)

Expectations

Has a diagnosis been made of the organization's general attitude toward

    ____ participation?

    ____ change?

    ____ pace of change?

    ____ belief in likelihood of changes being implemented?

____ Have clear messages been sent about what the project can realistically accomplish?

____ Has sufficient information about potential payoffs been disseminated so that people's expectations are high enough to be willing to get involved?

____ Have likely difficulties and a full timetable been made clear, so that expectations are not unrealistically high?

____ Has there been a chance for participants and others affected to check their expectations, test their assumptions, or voice their concerns?

Are participants at all levels clear about the extent of their

    ____ mandate?

    ____ authority?

    ____ budget, if any?

    ____ time commitment?

Project Participation

____ Is there enough organizational slack to allow participation of participants?

____ Is participation at all levels voluntary?

____ Are there mechanisms in place for informing all those eligible to volunteer?

____ Is the selection process fair?

    ____ perceived to be fair?

____ Are at least some participants' status high relative to their peers, to ensure that participation is seen as a reward?

____ Are at least some participants selected from among those who are low in opportunity/power/visibility?

____ Is there a clear way for supervisors of participants to stay informed and make suggestions?

Are the skills needed by participants to participate effectively

    ____ known?

    ____ known by them?

    ____ learnable through established/special means?

Checklist for Managing Corrective Action Projects (cont.)

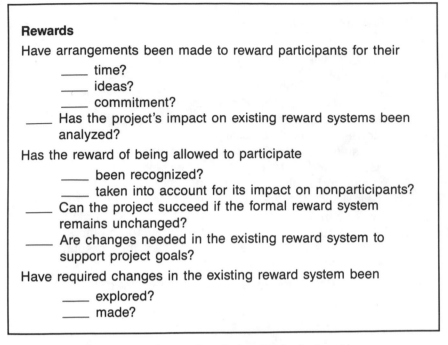

Rewards

Have arrangements been made to reward participants for their

_____ time?

_____ ideas?

_____ commitment?

_____ Has the project's impact on existing reward systems been analyzed?

Has the reward of being allowed to participate

_____ been recognized?

_____ taken into account for its impact on nonparticipants?

_____ Can the project succeed if the formal reward system remains unchanged?

_____ Are changes needed in the existing reward system to support project goals?

Have required changes in the existing reward system been

_____ explored?

_____ made?

Checklist for Managing Corrective Action Projects (cont.)

References

1. Kanter, R.M. "Work in a New America." *Daedalus* 107 (1978): 47-78.
2. Kanter, R.M. "A Good Job is Hard to Find." *Working Papers for a New Society* 7 (1979): 44-50
3. Cooper, M.R., B.S. Morgan, P.M. Foley, and L.B. Kaplan. "Changing Employee Values: Deepening Discontent?" *Harvard Business Review* 57 (1979): 117-125.
4. Pugh, D.S., D.J. Hickson, and C.R. Hinings. "An Empirical Taxonomy of Work Organizations." *Administrative Science Quarterly* 14 (1969): 115-126.
5. Davis, S.M., and P.R. Lawrence. *Matrix*. Reading, Mass.: Addison-Wesley, 1977.
6. Rothschild-Whitt, J. "The Collectivist Organization: An Alternative to Rational Bureaucratic Models." *American Sociological Review* 44 (1979): 509-527.
7. Miller, E.C. "The Parallel Organization Structure at General Motors: An Interview with Howard C. Carlson." *Personnel* 55, No. 4 (1978): 64-69.
8. Cohen, A.R. "The Human Dimension of Administrative Reform: Towards More Differentiated Strategies for Change." *Development and Change* (February 1971): 165-181.
9. Kanter, R.M. *Men and Women of the Corporation*. New York: Basic Books, 1977.
10. Kanter, R.M. "Access to Opportunity and Power: Measuring Institutional Racism/Sexism Inside Organizations." *In* R. Alvarex (ed.), *Social Indicators of Institutional Discrimination: Management and Research Tools*. San Francisco: Jossey-Bass, 1979.
11. *Survey: Conditions for Work Effectiveness*. Cambridge, Mass.: Goodmeasure, Inc., 1979.
12. *Instrument: Power Dimensions in Your Job*. Cambridge, Mass.: Goodmeasure, Inc., 1979.
13. Walton, R. "The Diffusion of New Work Structures: Explaining Why Success Didn't Take." *Organizational Dynamics* 3, No. 3 (1975): 2-22.
14. Gyllenhammar, P. *People at Work*. Reading, Mass.: Addison-Wesley, 1977.
15. Kanter, R.M., and B.A. Stein. "Where Leaders Can Lead: Toward New Organizational Structures." *The Wharton Magazine* 3, No. 4 (1979): 66-69.
16. Lawrence, P.R., and J.W. Lorsch. *Environment and Organization*. Boston: Graduate School of Business Administration, Harvard University, 1967.
17. Berg, I., M. Freedman, and M. Freeman. *Managers and Work Reform: A Limited Engagement*. New York: Free Press, 1978.